DINOSAURS

igloo

This edition published in 2009
by Igloo Books Ltd
Cottage Farm,
Sywell,
NN6 0BJ.
www.igloo-books.com

A copy of the British Library Cataloguing-in-Publication Data is available from the British Library.
10 9 8 7 6 5 4 3 2 1

ISBN: 978 1 84817 761 1

Front cover illustration: Malcolm Davis

Packaged by HL Studios, Long Hanborough, Oxfordshire
Printed and manufactured in China

CONTENTS

MYA - Million years ago
BYA - Billion years ago

In the text, some words have been highlighted in **bold**. You will find more information about what these mean in the glossary.

DINOSAUR TIMELINE

Massive volcanic eruptions cause mass extinctions, wiping out 90% of marine life and 70% of land life!

First dinosaurs evolve. They are mostly fairly small (no more than 6 m (20 ft)), bipedal and fast moving. Marine reptiles like Icthyosaurs and Plesiosaurs also evolve at this time.

Dinosaurs dominant. First mammals evolve.

Mesozoic era

248 MYA – 65 MYA

Triassic period	Jurassic period
248 MYA – 206 MYA	206 MYA – 144 MYA

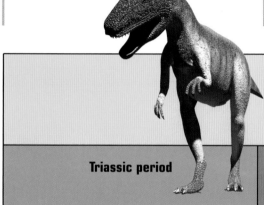

Sauropsids such as the archosaurs dominate. First cynodonts evolve.

Eoraptor
Coelophysis

Stegosaurus

Compsognathus
Diplodocus
Brachiosaurus

Apatosaurus
Kentrosaurus
Seismosaurus
Allosaurus

Megalosaurus

Age of dinosaurs. Dinosaurs are at their peak in size, variety and numbers and dominate every continent.

'K-T extinction'. End of the dinosaurs.

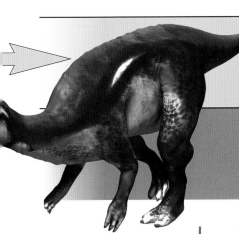

Mesozoic era

248 MYA – 65 MYA

Cretaceous period

144 MYA – 65 MYA

Hadrosaurus
Velociraptor
Protoceratops

Centrosaurus
Troodon
Tyrannosaurus
Triceratops
Ankylosaurus
Edmontosaurus

Giganotosaurus
Spinosaurus

Argentinosaurus
Nodosaurus

Deinonychus

Acrocanthosaurus

Iguanadon

Baryonyx

FULL TIMELINE

Oceans and atmosphere form. Earliest life forms in oceans.

Trilobites dominate seas. Still no land life.

Earliest land plants appear.

Insects flourish. First reptiles evolve. Shrubs, ferns and trees dominate land.

Massive volcanic eruptions cause mass extinctions, wiping out 90% of marine life and 70% of land life!

Precambrian time 4.5–3.9 BYA			Palaeozoic era 540 MYA–248 MYA					
Hadean eon	Archean eon	Proterozoic eon	Cambrian period	Ordovician period	Silurian period	Devonian period	Carboniferous period	Permian period

The Earth forms!

Sea plants begin photosynthesis.

First fish evolve.

Fish dominate oceans. Spiders and mites are first land creatures. First amphibians evolve. First forests form.

Synapsids, such as Dimetrodon and amphibians such as Eryops dominate land.

Dinosaurs dominate. First mammals evolve.

'K-T extinction' (see page 206). End of the dinosaurs.

Mammals such as horses, bats and whales evolve.

Most modern birds and mammals have evolved.

'Great Ice Age' Neanderthals and Homo sapiens, or modern humans, evolve. Smilodon (sabre-toothed tiger), mastodons and mammoths evolve.

Mesozoic era 248 MYA–65 MYA			Cenozoic era 65 MYA–NOW							
			Tertiary period (65 MYA – 1.8MYA)						Quaternary period (1.8MYA – NOW)	
Triassic period	Jurassic period	Cretaceous period	Paleocene epoch	Eocene epoch	Oligocene epoch	Miocene epoch	Pliocene epoch		Pleistocene epoch	Holocene epoch

Sauropsids such as the archosaurs dominate. First cynodonts such as Cynognathus evolve. Marine reptiles evolve.

Age of dinosaurs. Dinosaurs are at their peak in size, variety and numbers and dominate every continent.

Mammals dominate. Early carnivores evolve.

Creodonts evolve. Modern mammals become dominant.

Hominids, the ape-like ancestors of humans evolve. Thylacosmilus and other early sabre-tooths evolve.

Last ice age ends. Human civilisation develops.

EVOLUTION

The Earth, and all life on it, is constantly changing. Life had been on Earth for at least 3,260 million years before the dinosaurs appeared. The Palaeozoic era was from 540 to 250 million years ago, and was known as 'the age of ancient life'.

By 245–235 million years ago (the **Mesozoic era**) a large number of reptiles roamed the earth. Some of these were dinosaurs, including herbivorous **rhynchosaurs** and carnivorous archosaurs.

Dinosaurs appeared about 230 million years ago, during the Triassic period (see page 22). Their **evolution** spread over the Jurassic and Cretaceaous periods (see pages 24–27), a total of 165 million years.

Dinosaurs completely dominated the land in a way that no other group of animals had done. Eight hundred species have been identified so far. No one knows where they came from.

Extinction

About 65 million years ago (the end of the Cretaceous period), 70 per cent of living species, including the dinosaurs and flying reptiles suddenly became extinct. Crocodiles and many other reptiles survived.

Tsunami breaking wave

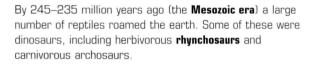

Dimetrodon

Archaeopteryx

Crocodile

The most popular explanation for this extinction is that an asteroid from space hit earth. There has been evidence of an enormous meteorite colliding with the Earth 65 million years ago. The meteorite may have been a single asteroid, bits from asteroid collisions, or debris from a comet. This would probably have thrown up an enormous amount of dust into the atmosphere which would have blocked out the sun and made the whole world dark for several months.

It might also have caused other natural disasters such as tsunamis and earthquakes. All plant life would have died, therefore plant eaters would not have been able to survive. In turn, carnivores would have had no food, causing them to die.

Other theories include a period of intense volcanic activity which may have caused changes such as global warming and effects on plant life. Another argument is that a drastic drop in sea level would have made the climate more extreme. It is difficult to imagine how this could have had such an effect. A third theory is that the climate changed enough to make earth too cold or hot for reptilian life, but this does not explain how some reptiles, such as crocodiles, survived.

The Cenozoic era began 65 million years ago and is often called the 'age of mammals', because mammals thrived at this time.

Scientists believe that birds are descendants of the dinosaurs. They may have come from small meat eaters such as Compsognathus (see page 62). You can see the similarity, especially when you compare the skeleton of dinosaurs to the skeleton of the oldest known bird, Archaeopteryx (see page 192), which lived about 140 million years ago.

ERYOPS

Primitive amphibian

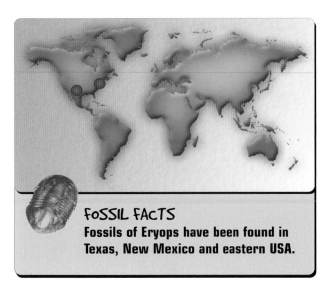

FOSSIL FACTS
Fossils of Eryops have been found in Texas, New Mexico and eastern USA.

Eryops was part of the Eryopidae family and probably lived during the Permian period (about 270 million years ago). This was a long time before the dinosaurs evolved. It was a primitive amphibian and looked a lot like the alligators that live today. The name Eryops means 'drawn-out face' because most of its skull was in front of its eyes.

Habitat

Because Eryops was an amphibian, this meant that it had to live near water (probably in swamps). This is so that it could lay its eggs. Amphibian eggs have no shells so they have to be laid in water or in a damp environment – otherwise they would dry out and die.

Appearance and diet

Although this meat eater had a short and stout body (it was about 1.5 m (5 ft) long), it was incredibly strong and was

probably one of the largest animals of its time. It had thick, strong bones, four short, but powerful legs and a short tail. Eryops also had a long and wide skull and lots of sharp teeth in its strong jaws.

Eryops' strong body was perfectly equipped for diving into the water and catching its prey. Its strength would also help to defend itself on land. Eryops probably ate mostly fish, small reptiles and other amphibians.

Predators

Eryops didn't have many predators, as they were one of the largest land animals, but they probably had to be wary of some of the Dimetrodon (see page 16), which moved faster than the Eryops on land.

In the water, the **Orthacanthus** may have preyed upon the Eryops, which would not have been able to move as quickly. However, some scientists believe the Eryops moved quicker in water than on land, where it may not even have been able to run.

MEGA FACTS

- Eryops had a primitive ear which allowed it to hear airborne sound.

- The fang-like teeth weren't actually used for chewing. Eryops would grasp its prey and then throw its head up and toss the meat farther backwards into its mouth, like alligators and crocodiles.

- Despite the fierce jaws and strong features, Eryops probably waited for fish to become stranded at the water's edge or for a small reptile to walk into its deadly path.

- Footprints were found in carboniferous rocks, which showed that Eryops walked in short and broad strides. This probably meant that they found walking very slow and difficult.

Dinosaur Data

PRONUNCIATION:	**AR**-EE-OPS
SUBORDER:	EUSKELIA
FAMILY:	ERYOPIDAE
DESCRIPTION:	ALLIGATOR-LIKE AMPHIBIAN
FEATURES:	SMALL YET POWERFUL
DIET:	FISH, SMALL REPTILES AND AMPHIBIANS

GERROTHORAX

Ancient type of amphibian

FOSSIL FACTS
Fossils have been found in Sweden and southern Germany.

Appearance

Gerrothorax was a type of **plagiosaurid**. This aquatic animal was thought to be 1 m (3 ft) long – that's about the same length as an adult seal. Gerrothorax looked a lot like a giant tadpole, but its body was flatter. Its head was short and wide and it had two small eyes that were really close together in the middle of its head.

Gerrothorax was not a dinosaur. It was an ancient type of amphibian that lived during the late Triassic period, about 200 million years ago. An amphibian is a kind of animal that is born from eggs, has bones and grows four legs. As babies they live in water and can then go on land. A frog is an amphibian.

Gerrothorax was a larval-like amphibian that lived in streams and lakes. Unlike frogs, it probably never left the water.

Like frogs, Gerrothorax had webbed feet. This was just on its back feet, probably to help propel it through the water. Gerrothorax also had a small tail.

Modern amphibians lose their gills when they grow older, Gerrothorax didn't. It had three pairs of gills throughout its life, meaning that it could live in water even as an adult.

Predators and diet

Gerrothorax was a meat eater and probably lay at the bottom of lakes, attracting prey with its mouth wide open, ready to catch whatever came swimming towards it. However, because of the flat head, it probably couldn't quickly snap its jaws as many fish do.

Gerrothorax may have had its own predators, which might explain why it was armoured above and below. Because of this heavy armour, it probably couldn't move very quickly.

MEGA FACTS

- Because its eyes were very close set on the top of its head, Gerrothorax could only look upwards so it would not have been able to see anything swimming underneath it.

- The very wide skull extended so much that it looked as if it had wings at each side.

Dinosaur Data

PRONUNCIATION:	GEH-ROH-**THOR**-AX
SUBORDER:	TREMATOSAURIA
FAMILY:	PLAGIOSAURIDAE
DESCRIPTION:	ANCIENT AMPHIBIAN
FEATURES:	FLAT, TADPOLE-LIKE BODY
DIET:	PROBABLY FISH

15

DIMETRODON

Four-footed sail-finned predator

ANCESTORS OF THE DINOSAURS

Dimetrodon had two different kinds of teeth – shearing teeth and sharp canines or incisors. This is one of the features of Dimetrodon that marks it out as an early synapsid (see page 208). The only surviving synapsids are mammals, a group which includes humans.

Appearance

Whilst its two kinds of teeth was one of the most important features of Dimetrodon, one of its most obvious features was the large sail-like fin that grew from its back. This fin could be up to 1 m (3 ft) high at its tallest point and was supported by a series of spines that grew out from the vertebrae of Dimetrodon's spinal cord.

FOSSIL FACTS
Dimetrodon fossils have been found in the USA.

Dimetrodon was a **pelycosaur** and lived several tens of millions of years before the earliest dinosaurs. The name Dimetrodon was given by Edward Drinker Cope in 1884 and means 'two measures teeth'.

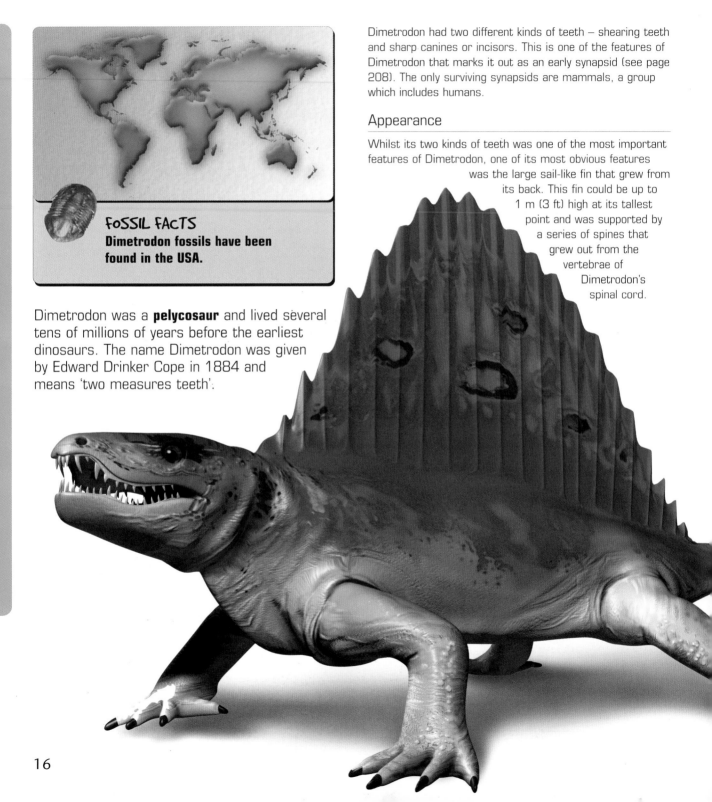

16

The fin could be used to control the heat of the body (a thermo-regulator) as well as being used to attract a mate or frightening other species by making them appear larger and more ferocious. It may have been brightly or multi-coloured but we can't be certain (as with many creatures we have discovered as fossils) because we can't tell what patterns or colours their skin as this detail simply doesn't exist in the fossils.

Diet

Dimetrodon lived mostly in swampy areas. Fossilised skeletons indicate that this creature could grow to about 3.5 m (11ft 6in.) long and probably weighed about 250 kg (550 lb), making it a ferocious predator compared to the other creatures of its time (the largest creature in the Permian period is believed to have been the Moschops, a 5 m (16.5 ft) long **herbivore**).

Built for speed

It is believed that Dimetrodon would have been the dominant **carnivore** in its environment, sitting at the top of the food chain with no predators. Dimetrodon had a long tail, a large head and four legs that sprawled out to the sides of its body, unlike dinosaurs whose legs were underneath their bodies. It's thought that this arrangement combined with its muscles made Dimetrodon a fast runner, enabling it to run down other slower moving creatures such as Eryops (see page 12).

The first Dimetrodon fossil was discovered in 1887.

MEGA FACTS

- **Dimetrodon's large sail-like fin was an excellent heat-exchanger.**

- **Dimetrodon is believed to have been a dominant carnivore with no predators.**

Dinosaur Data

PRONUNCIATION:	DIE-**MET**-ROE-DON
SUBORDER:	SPHENACODONTIA
FAMILY:	SPHENACODONTIDAE
DESCRIPTION:	LARGE CARNIVORE
FEATURES:	LARGE SAIL-LIKE FIN, 4 SIDE-SPRAWLING LEGS, LARGE HEAD WITH TWO TYPES OF TEETH, LONG TAIL
DIET:	OTHER PELYCOSAURS, INSECTS AND ANIMALS

EDAPHOSAURUS

Land-living reptile

Appearance

Edophosaurus looked similar to Dimetrodon (see page 16) because of its spiny back. This spine looked like a sail along its back. The sail was supported by bones in the vertebral column and scientists aren't sure what the sail was used for. Some believe that it was used to help the animal warm itself up more quickly. Others believe that it was used to attract a mate or warn others.

FOSSIL FACTS
Fossils of this creature have been found in Europe and North America.

The word Edaphosaurus means 'Earth lizard' in Greek. This reptile lived on land during the late Carboniferous and early Permian period, about 320 to 258 million years ago. This was a long time before the dinosaurs lived.

Edaphosaurus was a primitive **herbivore**. In fact, it was one of the earliest known plant-eating animals. It had flat teeth so it had to eat plants that it could easily crush. It probably lived near lakes or swamps.

It had a small, short and shallow skull and large eyes, with a wide body and thick tail. It was a **quadruped**. This quadruped was about 3.2 m (11 ft) long and weighed about 300 kg (660 lb).

We still know very little about the Edaphosaurus, as the only fossils that have ever been found only consist of a few fragments of its skeleton, including some of its spines.

Like the Dimetrodon, the Edaphosaurus was a **pelycosaur**. Pelycosaurs were small lizard-like animals that evolved into much larger and very different types. Some of the types were meat eaters and some were plant eaters like the Edophosaurus.

Pelycosaurs became extinct at beginning of the Permian period, long before the Triassic period when the dinosaurs evolved. Some of the types developed the sails on their backs and some did not. Eventually the synapsids evolved into the therapsids, which later led to the mammals.

MEGA FACTS

- In the morning, if Edaphosaurus stood with its sail at right angles to the rising sun, it would absorb the warmth quite quickly. This would raise Edaphosaurus' body temperature so that it could get going and find food quite quickly during the day.

- If it got too hot then by standing in a cooling breeze it could cool itself down quickly and effectively.

- Although nobody knows what colour its sail actually was it was thought to have been brightly-coloured and may have been used to attract a mate as some brightly-coloured birds do today.

- Although it could chew its food it also had a very large gut so it would swallow large amounts of partly-chewed leaves and stems and they would ferment in its gut to release the goodness.

Dinosaur Data

PRONUNCIATION:	AH-**DAF**-OH-**SAW**-US
SUBORDER:	PELYCOSAURIA
FAMILY:	EDAPHOSAURIDAE
DESCRIPTION:	A PRIMITIVE HERBIVORE
FEATURES:	SMALL AND STRONG
DIET:	PLANTS

WHAT ARE DINOSAURS?

Dinosaurs were a kind of prehistoric reptile. They ruled the Earth for more than 150 million years, during a period of time called the Mesozoic era. The first dinosaur appeared on Earth about 230 million years ago. They all died out about 65 million years ago.

Everything we know about the dinosaurs comes from the fossilised remains of their bones (and sometimes impressions of their skin, or footprints). This means scientists have very little to go on when they try to work out how dinosaurs lived. We cannot tell from fossils what colour a dinosaur's skin was, or what their voices sounded like. It is hard to tell how they

Some dinosaur myths

All dinosaurs were huge

Many were middle-sized or small. The smallest known dinosaur is Compsognathus (see page 62), which was only the size of a chicken.

All giant pre-historic animals were dinosaurs

Many other types of animal shared the Mesozoic era with the dinosaurs.
Pterosaurs flew, and marine reptiles like the ichthyosaurs swam in the oceans.

Some dinosaurs could fly, or swim

All dinosaurs lived on land. The pterosaurs and ichthyosaurs were not dinosaurs. Many scientists think that dinosaurs did eventually fly, though – by evolving into birds!

Dinosaurs were the biggest animals that ever lived

Although a plant-eating dinosaur called Argentinosaurus (see page 96) was the largest ever land animal, it was not as massive as a modern day giant, the blue whale.

Scientists have named about 800 kinds of dinosaurs so far and there must be many more fossils to find. New finds are made today almost every month – of course, not all of these are new species.

Most dinosaurs laid eggs and were cold-blooded. Apart from that, they were widely different in size, shape and speed. Some were **herbivores** and some **carnivores**. Some moved on all fours (these are called **quadrupeds**) and some on just their back legs (these are called **bipeds**).

behaved. Scientific detectives called **palaeontologists** study the fossil remains to learn as much as they can.

The name dinosaur means 'terrible lizard'. It comes from two Greek words: *deinos*, (terrifying) and *sauros* (lizard). The name was invented by Sir Richard Owen in 1842 (above left). Before that, people did not realise dinosaurs had once existed.

MEGA FACTS

- **Largest – Argentinosaurus, 35–45m (14–13 in.) long**

- **Smallest – Compsognathus, weighed 5.5kg (12 lb), and was only 60 cm (24 in.) long**

- **Widest – Ankylosaurus, 1.5 m (5 ft) wide**

- **Longest neck – Mamenchisaurus, neck was 10 m (33 ft) long**

- **Fastest – Ornithomiminee, ran at 64–85 km/ph (40–53 mph)**

- **First discovered – Iguanodon, found 1822**

- **Oldest – Eoraptor, lived 227 million years ago**

TRIASSIC PERIOD

Roughly 248 million years ago, about 95% of all species died out, including many marine animals. The cause might have been global cooling, volcanic eruptions, or a decrease in the continental shelf area during the formation of Pangaea. This catastrophic extinction and continental rearrangement opened the way for the rise of the dinosaurs and mammals.

The Triassic period was the first part of the **Mesozoic era**, the Age of Dinosaurs. It lasted from about 248 to 206 million years ago. During this period, dinosaurs and mammals evolved.

Eoraptor

Climate

There was no polar ice during this time, and the temperature was constantly warm. The continents were jammed together, forming the supercontinent **Pangaea**.

The formation of Pangaea, 220 million years ago, decreased the amount of shoreline, formed mountains, and gave the interior of the supercontinent a dry, desert-like terrain. The polar regions were moist and temperate. The climate was generally hot and dry, with strong seasonality.

Living things

There were no dinosaurs at the beginning of the period, but there were many amphibians, and some reptiles and dicynodonts (like Lystrosaurus). During the early Triassic period, corals appeared and ammonites recovered from the Permian extinction. Seed plants dominated the land.

Coral bed

Ammonite fossil

Mammals appear

During the late Triassic period, 220 million years ago, the first mammals appeared. Some scientists believe that mammals evolved from a group of extinct mammal-like reptiles, Theriodontia, which were therapsids. These primitive mammals were tiny and are thought to have been nocturnal.

Early dinosaurs

The very earliest dinosaurs were small, two-legged meat eaters, such as Coelophysis (see page 86) and Eoraptor (see page 84).

Eoraptor was a small, primitive, meat-eating dinosaur with sharp teeth.

The first plant eaters were prosaurapods like Massospondylus and Plateosaurus.

They could walk on two or four legs, presumably rearing up to get at higher plant life. Although they were small in comparison to the size of the later giant plant-eating dinosaurs, the prosauropods were by far the largest land animals of their time.

The rise of the dinosaurs during the late Triassic led to the decline of other, previously successful animal groups. Many sprawling reptiles and amphibians disappeared, and so did advanced mammal-like reptiles.

Late Triassic extinction

The Triassic period ended with a mass extinction accompanied by huge volcanic eruptions about 208–213 million years ago. The supercontinent Pangaea began to break apart. Roughly 35% of all animal families died out. Most of the early, primitive dinosaurs also became extinct, but other, more adaptive dinosaurs evolved in the Jurassic period.

No one is certain what caused this late Triassic extinction. Some possibilities include global cooling or an asteroid impact. This extinction allowed the dinosaurs to expand into many parts that were now unoccupied. Dinosaurs would become increasingly dominant, and remained that way for the next 150 million years.

Plateosaurus

23

JURASSIC PERIOD

After the Triassic period came the Jurassic period, which lasted from about 206 to 144 million years ago. Huge, long-necked dinosaurs appeared during the Jurassic period.

There was a minor mass extinction roughly 190–183 million years ago in which more than 80% of marine life (like many clams) and many other shallow-water species died out. The cause of this extinction is unknown.

In the middle of this period, the supercontinent Pangaea started to drift apart. A north-south rift formed and, by the late Jurassic period, Pangaea was split in two by huge rifts on the Earth's surface that created two new land areas, Laurasia in the north and Gondwana in the south. There must have been some land bridges between the two new supercontinents, because skeletons of dinosaurs have been found at opposite ends of the country from each other.

Allosaurus

Climate

At the beginning of the Jurassic period, the climate was hot and dry, but, when Pangaea began to break up, there were vast flooded areas, tropical forests, and coral reefs. The breakup of the land and the creation of large seas affected the global climate.

New dinosaurs

The tropical plant life which grew over huge areas brought about new dinosaurs, such as the saurapods like Apatosaurus (see page 100), Diplodocus (see page 98) and Brachiosaurus (see page 94).

Their long necks gave them access to the higher tree-top plants that other dinosaurs could not reach.

Apatosaurus

Stegosaurus

Many new groups also appeared. Meat-eating theropods like Allosaurus (see page 72) and Compsognathus (see page 62), and plated plant eaters like Stegosaurus (see page 116), evolved. Smaller coelurosaurs like Coelurus (see page 85) and Ornitholestes hunted lizards, mammals, and insects.

Sea life

In the Jurassic seas, there were abundant coral reefs, fish, ichthyosaurs (fish-like reptiles), giant marine crocodiles, and sharks. The air was dominated by the pterosaurs, the flying reptiles from the same original archosaur group as the dinosaurs. These were the largest vertebrates ever known to fly. Archaeopteryx also appeared, the earliest known bird, with many dinosaur features, proving that birds evolved from dinosaurs.

In terms of sheer size and geography, the Jurassic period is the high point of the dinosaur era. The upright way of walking allowed the dinosaurs to develop different body shapes and sizes to take full advantage of the environment. By the end of the period, dinosaurs had expanded to fill virtually almost every usable part of the land surface.

There was a minor mass extinction toward the end of the period. During this extinction, most of the stegosaurid and enormous sauropod dinosaurs died out. No one knows what caused this extinction.

Diplodocus

25

CRETACEOUS PERIOD

The Cretaceous period, lasting from 144 to 65 million years ago, was the last part of the Mesozoic era. Most of the known dinosaurs lived during the Cretaceous period. During this time, mammals flourished; flowering plants evolved and changed the landscape radically. There was a high level of tectonic activity (continental plate movement) and accompanying volcanic activity.

The Cretaceous period ended 65 million years ago with the extinction of the dinosaurs and many other prehistoric life forms. This mass extinction was the second most extensive in the history of the earth.

Geography and climate change

The break-up of the supercontinent **Pangaea** into separate continents was underway. By the end of the period the outlines of continents were roughly those that we recognise today. In the first half of the Cretaceous period, temperatures were warm and global sea levels were high.

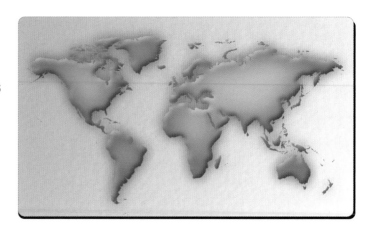

During the mid-Cretaceous period, many mountain ranges were formed, including California's Sierra Nevadas, the Rocky Mountains in the western USA, and the European Alps. The sea levels rose, covering about one-third of the land area.

Towards the end of the period, there was a drop in sea level, causing greater temperature extremes. At the end of the Cretaceous period, there were severe climate changes, lowered sea levels, and high volcanic activity.

Rocky mountains, USA

Cretaceous dinosaurs

We know of more different species from the late Cretaceous Period than we do from all the other dinosaur periods put together. Huge carnivores like Tyrannosaurus Rex (see page 54) and Giganotosaurus (see page 56) appeared, as did Triceratops (see page 136) and many others.

There was a tremendous diversity in dinosaur species. The effect of the land breakup, as well as new plant life in the form of flowering plants (angiosperms), meant that dinosaurs started to become isolated from each other on separate continents. The same species of dinosaurs developed in different ways, depending on the areas they lived in. For example, there were noticeable differences between the North American hadrosaurs and the groups in China or Africa.

Other cretaceous life

Mammals were flourishing during this period, and many creatures such as snakes and moths appeared.

Flowering plants, like magnolia, developed and radically changed the landscape. The earliest fossils of birds resembling pelicans, flamingos, and sandpipers were from the Cretaceous period.

Mass extinction

At the end of the Cretaceous period, about 65 million years ago, a mass extinction wiped out the dinosaurs (except for the birds) and many other animals. The primary cause of the extinction is thought to be an asteroid impact, but there are a lot of other theories, including volcanoes and climate changes due to continental drift (see page 10). Although this extinction was huge, it was small when compared to the extinction which preceded the existence of the dinosaurs. The age of reptiles came to an end; the age of mammals was about to begin.

DINOSAUR BRAINS

Some scientists believe that dinosaurs were dull, stupid creatures, and whilst this might be partially true for the large plant eaters, this was not the case for the smaller, highly-active predators who had to think and move quickly in order to capture enough prey to stay alive. Luckily dinosaurs had tough, bony skulls which meant that their skulls were well preserved, and we can find out about their brains.

Small brains

Some of the slow plant eaters, like Apatosaurus (see page 100), had giant bodies but tiny brains. For example, Stegosaurus (see page 116) had a brain the size of a walnut that weighed just 70 g (3 oz). In relation to its size, Stegosaurus had the smallest brain of any dinosaur. However, Stegosaurus also had a secondary nerve centre (sometimes incorrectly called a second brain) near the base of its spine that helped it move its rear legs and tail.

These dinosaurs belonged to a group called the **sauropods** that didn't need much of a brain to survive. All they had to do was eat plants – they didn't have to hunt for food or look out for predators. Another **herbivore**, Triceratops (a horned dinosaur or **ceratopsian**), only had a 300 g (12 oz) brain in a body of 6,000–9,000 kg (6–9 tons).

More intelligent dinosaurs

Dinosaurs which lived in herds, such as the plant-eating hadrosaurs (see page 104), survived through herd communication and so used their brains much more. It is thought that some hadrosaurs, such as Parasaurolophus (see page 180), were able to use their distinctive head crests as sound-making devices, blowing air through the internal tubes to produce a noise. This would have been ideal as an alarm to the herd when a predator was spotted.

Hadrosaurs also had no armour, so were much more intelligent as they constantly had to be on the lookout for danger from predators.

Parasaurolophus

28

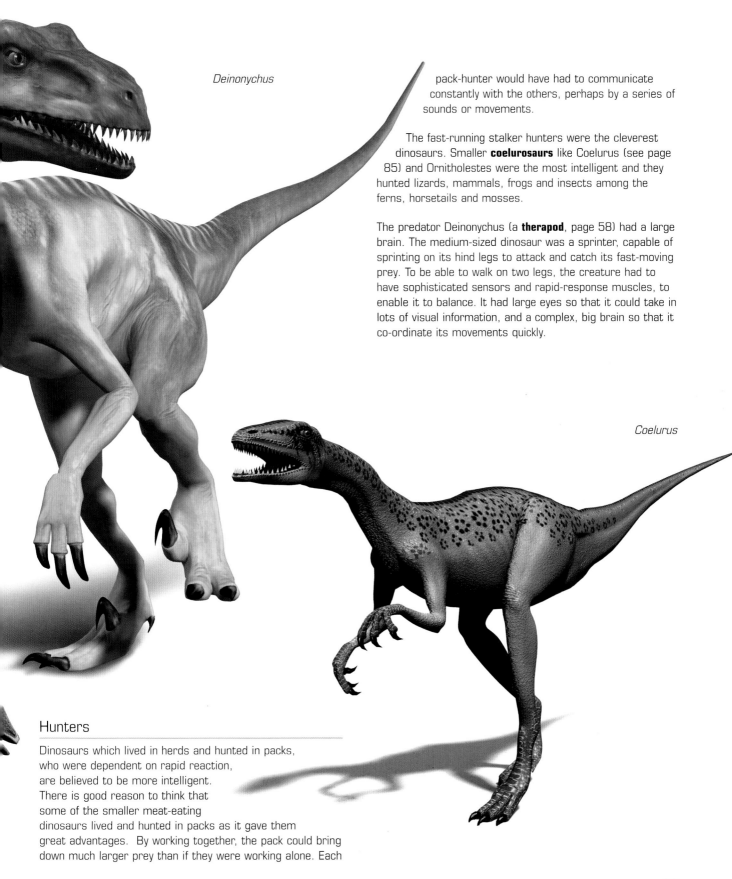

Deinonychus

pack-hunter would have had to communicate constantly with the others, perhaps by a series of sounds or movements.

The fast-running stalker hunters were the cleverest dinosaurs. Smaller **coelurosaurs** like Coelurus (see page 85) and Ornitholestes were the most intelligent and they hunted lizards, mammals, frogs and insects among the ferns, horsetails and mosses.

The predator Deinonychus (a **therapod**, page 58) had a large brain. The medium-sized dinosaur was a sprinter, capable of sprinting on its hind legs to attack and catch its fast-moving prey. To be able to walk on two legs, the creature had to have sophisticated sensors and rapid-response muscles, to enable it to balance. It had large eyes so that it could take in lots of visual information, and a complex, big brain so that it co-ordinate its movements quickly.

Coelurus

Hunters

Dinosaurs which lived in herds and hunted in packs, who were dependent on rapid reaction, are believed to be more intelligent. There is good reason to think that some of the smaller meat-eating dinosaurs lived and hunted in packs as it gave them great advantages. By working together, the pack could bring down much larger prey than if they were working alone. Each

SENSES

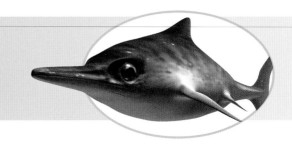

Saurornithoides

page 54) and Giganotosaurus (see page 56), the largest meat-eating dinosaur of all time, had a keen sense of smell and good eyesight. They could possibly have smelt potential prey from some distance away. They could also pick up the scent of dead bodies, from a long distance, from which they could scavenge meat.

It is thought that some dinosaurs' noses had a special scent gland that would have been used to release hormones into the air. The hormones could have been carried lomg distance and may have been used to attract a mate.

It is hard to tell what dinosaurs were like because humans haven't been able to watch them and observe how they behave, but scientists can work out information about their senses from evidence left behind. Like all living things, dinosaurs had five senses; taste, touch, sight, sound and smell.

Touch

A dinosaur's sense of touch was probably not very well developed, because of their thick skin. Their sense of taste was more well developed, although big eaters like Allosaurus (see page 72) probably didn't taste much of their meal when eating as they eat so fast!

Taste and smell

The senses of taste and smell were controlled by the same part of the dinosaur's brain, and were closely linked. They were used by hunters and hunted to keep track of each other, by some plant eaters to tell the difference between certain foods and, in many species, as part of the mating process.

The predators were probably able to smell very well, in order to hunt their prey. Both Tyrannosaurus Rex (see

Troodon

Vision and hearing

Most dinosaurs had good side vision, with eyes set at the sides of their heads, but because their eyes didn't face forward, they weren't very good at judging distances. Smaller meat-eating dinosaurs had good vision and good co-ordination, which meant they were very successful in stalking and chasing smaller creatures.

Troodon (see page 82) had exceptionally large eyes, based on the size of the eye sockets, and the biggest brain of any dinosaur relative to its body size.

Coelophysis (see page 86), a small meat-eating **therapod** dinosaur, had a large brain in comparison to its reptilian ancestors, and its senses were finely tuned. It had excellent eyesight and hearing that, in combination with its fast legs, long neck, short arms and sharp claws, would have helped it catch fish, small reptiles and other prey.

Dinosaurs did not have exterior ear flaps like mammals but heard through holes set far back in the head behind their eyes. It was probably herding dinosaurs, with their strong need to communicate, that had the most acute sense of hearing. Hadrosaurs (see page 104) display the only real evidence so far of being able to make noises, with a variety of nasal trumpets and air sacs. However, like many modern land animals, dinosaurs would probably have made noises if they needed to, for example to attract a mate, defend their territory or warn of danger.

Giganotosaurus

31

HEADS AND TAILS

Every dinosaur was made up of the same basic skeletal parts, but heads and tails varied in appearance and function.

The biggest dinosaurs often had very small heads. A Brachiosaurus (see page 94) may have eaten up to a tonne of plants every day just to stay alive. It had a head not much larger than a horse's and teeth which didn't chew. Torosaurus was also a **herbivore** but had the most powerful jaw muscles of any known dinosaur. These, when combined with its sharp beak and around 600 teeth, allowed it to slice through any plant, including tree branches.

Skills

The skull differed from dinosaur to dinosaur, depending on what it was needed for. Deinonychus (see page 58) had a lightweight skull.

Combined with its slim neck, this was ideal for quick, snapping bites. Tyrannosaurus Rex (see page 54), had a large head which was heavily reinforced with bone and shock-absorbing muscle to withstand the impact of crashing into a victim with mouth open and then delivering a crushing bite. Its jaw could be 1.2 m (4 ft) long and the many teeth would attack an animal. It had to swallow its food whole, and could probably gulp up to 70 kg (154 lb) of meat in one go.

Styracosaurus

Deinonychus skull

Dinosaurs had different markings and body parts to distinguish them from each other, compete with other males and find a mate. Styracosaurus (see page 150) had an impressive head structure. Its round bony frill was actually longer than the skull itself, and decorated round the outer edge with long spikes. By tilting its head forward and swinging it from side to side, Styracosaurus could produce an impressive display of size and aggression to frighten off other males and display their strength.

Protecting the head and neck

As the head and neck were such a vulnerable part for a dinosaur, it was important that it could be protected. Some dinosaurs, such as Euoplocephalus, had studs and plates to protect them. Its head was heavily armoured, with slabs of reinforcing bone over all exposed surfaces and triangular side studs above and below the eyes. The eyelids were made of bone, closing like steel shutters, to deflect the gouging claw of an attacker.

Tails

The end of Diplodocus' tail was so long and thin that some scientists believe it was used like a bullwhip for defence. Although quite a few **saurapod** tracks have been found around the world, there are very few that show evidence of tail-drag marks. Scientists have decided that the sauropods kept their tails up off the ground when they walked.

Ankylosaurus (see page 118), had a heavily-armoured tail. Ankylosaurus, if attacked, could use its club-like tail as a weapon, swinging it from side to side like a knight's mace. The club itself was a weighty mass of fused bony tissue that was quite capable of smashing through the leg bones of even the largest dinosaurs.

Tyrannosaurus Rex skull

Ankylosaurus

ICHTHYOSAURUS

Aquatic hunter/killer

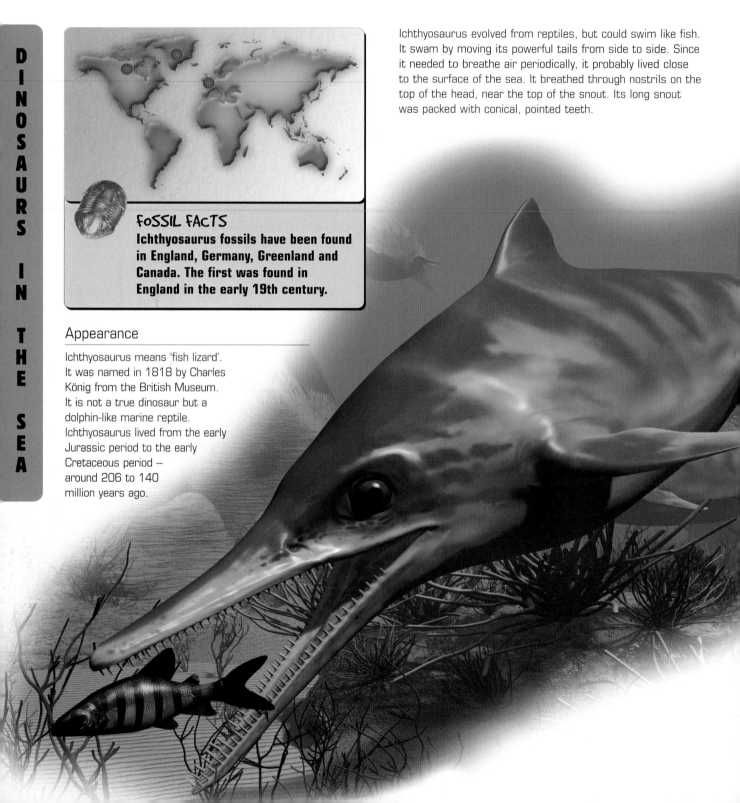

FOSSIL FACTS
Ichthyosaurus fossils have been found in England, Germany, Greenland and Canada. The first was found in England in the early 19th century.

Ichthyosaurus evolved from reptiles, but could swim like fish. It swam by moving its powerful tails from side to side. Since it needed to breathe air periodically, it probably lived close to the surface of the sea. It breathed through nostrils on the top of the head, near the top of the snout. Its long snout was packed with conical, pointed teeth.

Appearance

Ichthyosaurus means 'fish lizard'. It was named in 1818 by Charles König from the British Museum. It is not a true dinosaur but a dolphin-like marine reptile. Ichthyosaurus lived from the early Jurassic period to the early Cretaceous period – around 206 to 140 million years ago.

Reproduction and diet

Ichthyosaurus was smooth-skinned and streamlined, and had limbs (flippers) like large paddles to balance it in the water – the front 'paddles' were twice as large as the back ones. Its eyes were unusually large, and surrounded by a strong ring of bone. A fish-like tail helped propel it, and a dorsal fin provided extra balance.

Ichthyosaurus gave birth to live young – we know this because fossils have been found showing baby Ichthyosaurus bones in the abdomen of adults. Fossils have also helped us learn about the diet of Ichthyosaurus – the hard hooks found on the tentacles of squid cannot be digested and so remained in the belly; one fossil of an Ichthyosaurus showed it had swallowed at least 1,500 squid while alive.

The first complete ichthyosaurus fossil remains were found at Lyme Regis in England, by a girl called Mary Anning, in the early 19th century. Mary Anning made a living from collecting, studying and selling fossils.

MEGA FACTS

- Most were around 2 m (6 ft) long, though some were as big as 9 m (30 ft). An average weight for these dolphin-like creatures was 90 kg (200 lb).

- We know Ichthyosaurus must have moved fast to hunt its prey, because the remains of a fast-swimming fish called Pholidophorus have been found in fossilised Ichthyosaurus droppings. It could swim at speeds of up to 40 km/h (25 mph).

- Ichthyosaurus skeletons found at Holzmaden (Germany) were so well preserved that scientists could see outlines of skin as well as bones.

- In 2000, an Ichthyosaurus skeleton, believed to be almost a perfect specimen, was revealed as a fake when it was cleaned. It had been made in the Victorian age from the bones of two different creatures and some bones made out of plaster.

Icthyosaurus fossil

Dinosaur Data

PRONUNCIATION:	IK-THEE-OH-**SAWR**-US
SUBORDER:	ICHTHYOSAURIA
FAMILY:	ICHTHYOSAURIDAE
DESCRIPTION:	OCEAN-DWELLING PREDATOR
FEATURES:	ENORMOUS EYES, FOUR CRESCENT-SHAPED FLIPPERS, DORSAL FIN
DIET:	FISH, OCTOPUS AND OTHER SEA-DWELLING CREATURES

ELASMOSAURUS

Long-necked marine reptile

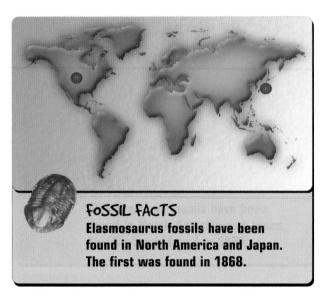

FOSSIL FACTS
Elasmosaurus fossils have been found in North America and Japan. The first was found in 1868.

Unfortunately, when Cope assembled his Elasmosaurus skeleton for display, he placed the head on the wrong end! His rivals soon pointed out his mistake, and made fun of him for it for the rest of his career.

Appearance

The neck of Elasmosaurus contained more than 70 **vertebrae**. Elasmosaurus was the largest of a type of marine reptile called **plesiosaurs**. It had a large body, four long, broad paddles for limbs, and a small head with sharp, interlocking teeth.

The long neck may have enabled Elasmosaurus to feed in a number of different ways.

Elasmosaurus means 'thin-plated lizard' – the name refers to the plate-like bones in the creature's pelvic girdle. It lived 88–65 million years ago, and swam in the great inland sea that covered much of the western part of North America in those times. Its body was dwarfed by its long thin neck and shorter tail.

Elasmosaurus was named by Edward Drinker Cope, who discovered the first fossil.

Dinosaur Data

PRONUNCIATION:	EE-**LAZ**-MOH-SAWR-US
SUBORDER:	PLESIOSAURIOID
FAMILY:	ELASMOSAURIDAE
DESCRIPTION:	HUGE, SLOW-SWIMMING MARINE REPTILE
FEATURES:	EXTREMELY LONG NECK, TINY HEAD
DIET:	FISH AND OTHER SMALL MARINE CREATURES

It may have floated along on the surface, stretching down to the sea bottom to catch fish and other marine creatures. It could also make attacks upward at shoals of fish while its body was much lower down in the water. It could move slowly and stealthily toward them, then attack with a quick darting movement. The small size of its head and its narrow neck meant it could only eat and swallow smaller creatures. Elasmosaurus fossils have been found with rounded pebbles in their stomachs – perhaps they swallowed these to aid their digestion or to help them sink further down into the water.

Elasmosaurus is believed to have been a very slow swimmer. It would have travelled long distances to find safe mating and breeding grounds.

Reproduction

For a long time, it was assumed that Elasmosaurus laid eggs like most reptiles, crawling ashore to lay its eggs on land. However, many scientists now think that Elasmosaurus gave birth to live young, which it raised until they could look after themselves in the predator-filled ocean. Elasmosaurus may have travelled together in small groups to protect their young.

MEGA FACTS

- About 14 m (46 ft) long, Elasmosaurus was the longest of the plesiosaurs.

- Pictures often show Elasmosaurus holding its head high above the surface of the water at the end of its long neck. Actually, gravity would have made it impossible for it to lift much more than its head above water.

- Elasmosaurus, with its long snake-like neck, is one of the candidates for the Loch Ness Monster (see page 228).

KRONOSAURUS

Giant short-necked marine reptile

DINOSAURS IN THE SEA

Kronosaurus means 'Kronos's lizard'. It had a short neck, four flippers, a huge head with powerful jaws and a short, pointed tail.

Kronosaurus was a marine reptile called a pliosaur (a type of **plesiosaur**). It was heavier, faster and fiercer than most plesiosaurs. It lived in the seas that covered parts of Australia, and breathed air. It swam with four powerful paddle-like flippers and may have been able to climb out onto land and move around a little. It probably had to leave water to lay its eggs in nests it would dig in the sand.

Diet

Kronosaurus ate other sea creatures such as ammonites and squid. Rounded teeth at the back of its powerful jaws enabled Kronosaurus to crunch up tough shells and crush bone.

The fossilised remains of turtles and even smaller plesiosaurs have been found in the stomachs of Kronosaurus fossils, and long-necked plesiosaur skeletons have been found with Kronosaurus-like toothmarks on the bones. Like Elasmosaurus (see page 36), small stones have been found in Kronosaurus stomachs which might have helped them grind up their food during digestion.

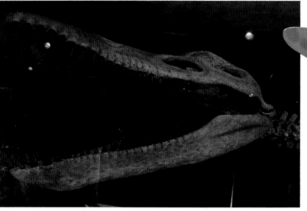

Kronosaurus skeleton

FOSSIL FACTS
Kronosaurus fossils have been found in Australia and Columbia – the first were found in Queensland, Australia by A. Crombie in 1889.

Kronosaurus

Dinosaur Data

PRONUNCIATION:	CROW-NO-SAWR-US
DESCRIPTION:	POWERFUL AQUATIC PREDATOR
FEATURES:	HUGE HEAD, POWERFUL JAWS
DIET:	**CARNIVORE**; ATE OTHER MARINE CREATURES

Kronosaurus may have been able to 'scent' under water for its prey — it had internal nostrils where water could enter, and external ones further back on the top of its skull for water to exit. While the water passed from one set to the other, scent particles could be detected.

Appearance

Kronosaurus had an enormous head as skulls have been found measuring 3 m (10 ft). As their whole body length is believed to be only around

9 m (30 ft), this means their head took up a third of it!

It was originally thought to be much longer, earning it the title of 'largest ever plesiosaur', but recent studies have led scientists to downsize their image of Kronosaurus. The team of scientists who mounted the first specimen for display had to fill in many 'gaps' in the skeleton — they gave their mounted Kronosaurus too many vertebrae and so made it longer than it should have been.

MEGA FACTS

- Fast and fierce — one of the top predators of the ancient ocean.

- Some of Kronosaurus' teeth were 25 cm (10 in.) long, although much of this length was embedded in the jawbone.

- When Kronosaurus fossils were first discovered in 1889, they were believed to come from an ichthyosaur. Kronosaurus did not get a name of its own until 1924.

- When the first Kronosaurus skeleton was assembled, the specimen was in such a bad state that the team had to fill in many details using plaster and their own imagination. This led to the creature being nicknamed the 'Plasterosaurus'!

TYLOSAURUS

Gigantic marine predator

DINOSAURS IN THE SEA

FOSSIL FACTS

Tylosaurus fossils have been found in North America and New Zealand. The first fossils were found in Kansas (USA) in 1869. The yellow dots show where material which may relate to Tylosaurus has also been found – in Angola, South Africa and Japan.

The name Tylosaurus comes from the Greek words *tylos* (knob or protuberance) and *sauros* (lizard). It is named after its remarkable long and almost cylindrical snout that has a rounded, bony end. Tylosaurus was a marine reptile known as a **mosasaur**. It was one of the most gigantic of the mosasaurs, growing up to 12 m (39 ft) long – that's as long as a double-decker bus!

Dinosaur Data

PRONUNCIATION:	**TIE**-LOW-**SAWR**-US
SUBORDER:	LACERTILIA
FAMILY:	MOSASAURIDAE
DESCRIPTION:	MASSIVE SEA PREDATOR
FEATURES:	POWERFUL TAIL, LONG ROUNDED SNOUT
DIET:	FISH, MARINE CREATURES, FLIGHTLESS BIRDS

Dinosaur Data

PRONUNCIATION:	CAW-**DIP**-TER-IKS
SUBORDER:	THEROPODA
FAMILY:	CAUDIPTERIDAE
DESCRIPTION:	LONG-LEGGED FEATHERED DINOSAUR
FEATURES:	DISTINCTIVE TAIL PLUME, FEATHERS AND WING-LIKE ARMS
DIET:	SMALL FISH

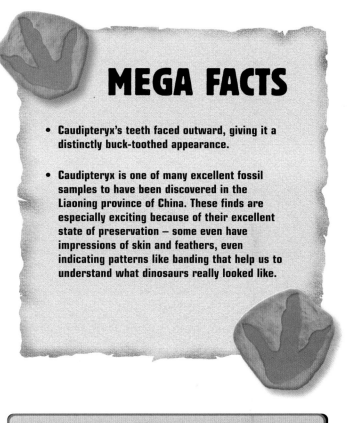

MEGA FACTS

- Caudipteryx's teeth faced outward, giving it a distinctly buck-toothed appearance.

- Caudipteryx is one of many excellent fossil samples to have been discovered in the Liaoning province of China. These finds are especially exciting because of their excellent state of preservation — some even have impressions of skin and feathers, even indicating patterns like banding that help us to understand what dinosaurs really looked like.

Evolution of Birds

Most scientists now accept that birds evolved from dinosaurs. However, some believe that all birds descended from a creature called Archaeopteryx (see page 192). Others believe that modern birds evolved from the maniraptors, a group whose early members included Caudipteryx and whose later members included Velociraptor (see page 66) and Deinonychus (see page 58). These later members had evolved the swivelling wrist bone joint that is necessary for flight.

Caudipteryx's feathers and wing-like arms suggest that it might be the missing link in the evolution of birds from dinosaurs!

ARCHAEOPTERYX

Winged and feathered bipedal carnivore

FOSSIL FACTS
Fossils have been found in Bavaria, in Germany.

Bird-like features	Dinosaur-like features
Feathered wings with reduced finger	Claws on wings, could be used to grasp
Wishbone	Teeth
Bird-like brain	Long bony tail
Hollow bones	Jaws (not a beak!)
Feathers on body and tail	

This table gives details of the features that Archaeopteryx shared with birds and dinosaurs.

In 2004, an experiment was carried out at the National History Museum in London to try to answer this question. Scanning equipment was used to scan the brain case of an Archaeopteryx skull. The brain shape was much more like that of a modern bird than the brain of a dinosaur.

Archaeopteryx means 'ancient feather'. It was named by Hermann von Meyer in 1861. Archaeopteryx is often said to be a link between dinosaurs and birds.

Appearance

Archaeopteryx was magpie-sized, weighing around 325 g (12 oz). It had short, broad wings and a long tail and neck. Its jaws were lined with sharp cone-shaped teeth. It had long legs, with long thighs and short calves. Its wings, body and tail were feathered. Its large eyes would have given it excellent vision. It had feathers and wings like a bird, but teeth, skeleton and claws like a dinosaur.

In 2005, a particularly well-preserved fossil specimen was studied. The second toe could be stretched much more t han the rest, rather like the special 'retractable' claws of Velociraptor (see page 66). The hind toe was not 'reversed' like a thumb on a grasping hand, and so Archaeopteryx could not have used it to cling onto branches.

Could Archaeopteryx fly?

Scientists have argued over whether or not this animal could fly ever since the first Archaeopteryx fossil was found. If it could fly, did it just flap its wings weakly, or fly strongly?

Permian period	Triassic period	Jurassic period	Cretaceous period
90-248 million years ago)	(248-176 million years ago)	(176-130 million years ago)	(130-66 million years ago)

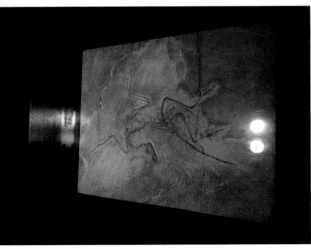

Archaeopteryx fossil

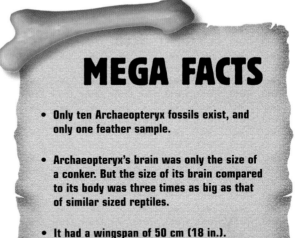

MEGA FACTS

- Only ten Archaeopteryx fossils exist, and only one feather sample.

- Archaeopteryx's brain was only the size of a conker. But the size of its brain compared to its body was three times as big as that of similar sized reptiles.

- It had a wingspan of 50 cm (18 in.).

- There were flying dinosaurs before and after Archaeopteryx, but they had skin, not feathers, on their wings.

The areas controlling vision and movements were enlarged, just like a bird's, and the inner ear (which controls balance) was also like a bird's. It was a brain designed for flight and balance!

Dr Angela Milner, who carried out the study, believes this is strong evidence that Archaeopteryx could and did fly. Most scientists now agree that archaeopteryx *could* fly, but was a weak flyer.

Dinosaur Data

PRONUNCIATION:	ARK-EE**OP**-TER-IKS
SUBORDER:	THERAPODA
FAMILY:	ARCHAEOPTERIDAE
DESCRIPTION:	FEATHERED BIPEDAL CARNIVORE
FEATURES:	FEATHERED WINGS
DIET:	INSECTS, SMALL CREATURES

PTERANODON INGENS

Winged and toothless flying reptile

FLYING DINOSAURS

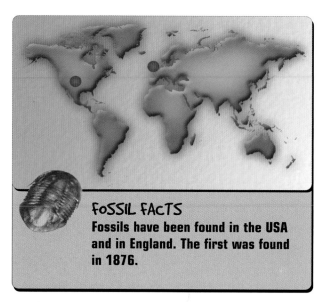

FOSSIL FACTS
Fossils have been found in the USA and in England. The first was found in 1876.

Dinosaur Data

PRONUNCIATION:	TER-AN-O-DON
SUBORDER:	PTERODACTYLOIDEA
FAMILY:	PTERADONTIDAE
DESCRIPTION:	CARNIVORE
FEATURES:	HUGE WINGSPAN
DIET:	FISH, MOLLUSCS, CRABS, INSECTS

It probably looked more like a huge bat than a bird with large soft hair covered membranes for wings. The membrane itself was very thin but extremely strong and stretched out between the body and the tops of its legs. These flying reptiles did not have any feathers.

Pteranodon lived at the same time as Tyrannosaurus Rex. It was not a true dinosaur but was related to them.

Pteranodon had a wing span of up to 9–10 m (30–33 ft) and weighed around 20–25 kg (44–55 lb).

194

It would have been able to walk on the ground but, once in the air, Pteranodon would have looked like a huge glider. Pteranodon could fly long distances using its large light-weight wings; it would have taken advantage of rising thermals to soar over the swampy forest below.

MEGA FACTS

- It used the large bony crest on its head to steer when flying.

- Their brightly-coloured crests were larger in the male and were used for attracting females and indicating readiness to mate.

- Their lower jaw was over 1m (3 ft) in length.

- They would have been agile, elegant and quite fast when flying, reaching speeds up to 48 km/h (30 mph).

Diet

It had no teeth but was **carnivorous**. Fossil skeletons found near the edge of the sea show that fish was probably an important part of its diet. Its scoop-like beak would have helped it to swoop down to catch fish straight from near the surface of the water. Its excellent eyesight would have helped it to see fish in the water as it flew above the surface.

HESPERORNIS

Flightless toothed marine dinosaur

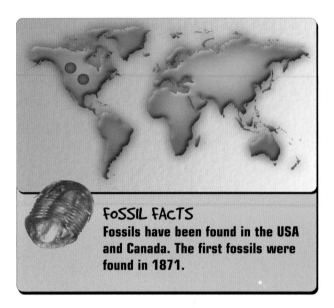

FOSSIL FACTS
Fossils have been found in the USA and Canada. The first fossils were found in 1871.

Hesperornis means 'western bird'. It was named in 1871 by the **palaeontologist** Othniel C. Marsh. The discovery of Hesperornis was very important, because it filled a big gap in the fossil history of birds.

Hesperornis is part of a group of dinosaurs called the hesperornithiforms. These were the only true marine dinosaurs of the whole Mesozoic era. Dinosaurs that lived in the sea seem to have lived only in the northern hemisphere and were flightless diving birds. They would have dived to catch fish.

Appearance

Hesperornis looked a lot like a bird with teeth. It grew to about 1.5 m (5 ft) long and it had small and useless wings (which scientists call *vestigal* wings). It had sprawling back legs, set very far back on the body. These long legs ended in webbed feet. It had a big head on the end of a long neck. Its long beak was set with simple, sharp teeth along its bottom jaw, and at the back of its upper jaw.

A different kind of hesperornithiform, called Parahesperornis, has been found showing the imprinted remains of thick, hairy feathers. It is likely that Hesperornis, too, had such feathers. They would not have helped it fly, but would have done a good job of keeping it warm.

In the water, Hesperornis was a powerful swimmer and diver. Unlike modern flightless birds like penguins, it did not use its wings as well as its feet to push itself through the water. Its wings were tiny and of no use, but its back

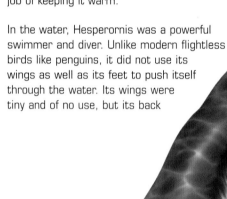

Dinosaur Data

PRONUNCIATION:	**HES**-PER-**OR**-NIS
SUBORDER:	ODONTORNITHES
FAMILY:	HESPERORNITHIDAE
DESCRIPTION:	FLIGHTLESS TOOTHED DIVING BIRD
FEATURES:	VESTIGAL WINGS, TOOTHED BEAK
DIET:	FISH, SQUID, AMMONITES

legs were powerful. The wings may have been useful for steering when diving underwater. It had dense (heavy) bones that made it less buoyant and helped it to dive. Its sleek, feathered body was well designed for moving smoothly through the water.

On land, Hesperornis was awkward and clumsy. Thanks to the position of its hip bones and back legs, it may not even have been able to stand up and waddle about on dry land. It would have moved on land by sliding about on its belly, pushing with those strong back legs. It probably only went up on land to nest and lay eggs. For safety, it probably nested in groups, and chose inaccessible, rocky spots.

MEGA FACTS

- Hesperornis remains have been found in the fossilised stomachs of mosasaur (see page 42) skeletons.

- Hesperornis was the largest of the flightless diving birds of the late Cretaceous period.

- Unable to fly or walk, Hesperornis was in danger from predators both in the water and on land.

197

RHAMPHORYNCUS

Flying reptile

**F
L
Y
I
N
G

D
I
N
O
S
A
U
R
S**

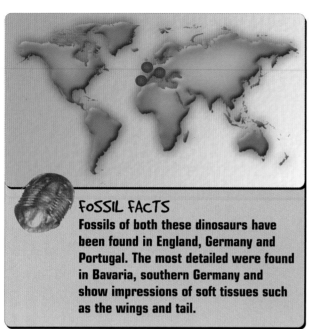

FOSSIL FACTS
Fossils of both these dinosaurs have been found in England, Germany and Portugal. The most detailed were found in Bavaria, southern Germany and show impressions of soft tissues such as the wings and tail.

Rhamphorhynchus was a pterosaur, which lived during the late Jurassic period. It had a wingspan up to 1.75 m (6 ft). The wings were made of thin skin stretched between an elongated finger from its hand, down to its ankle.

Rhamphorhynchus had a long, thin and pointed tail. At the end of its tail it had a flap of skin, which was diamond shaped. This helped with its balance in flight.

Rhamphorhynchus also had long and thin jaws with incredibly sharp teeth, probably for catching fish. It is believed that one of the ways Rhamphorhynchus hunted was by dragging its beak in the water in the hope of coming into contact with fish, then it would snap its needle-sharp teeth shut and toss the food into its throat pouch. It probably wouldn't have hunted on land as it only had tiny legs, which would have made it a poor runner.

Dinosaur Data

PRONUNCIATION:	**RAM-FOR-INK-US**
SUBORDER:	RHAMPHORHYNCHOIDEA
FAMILY:	RHAMPHORHYNCHIDAE
DESCRIPTION:	FLYING REPTILE
FEATURES:	BIRD-LIKE MEAT EATER
DIET:	FISH, MOLLUSKS, INSECTS

PTEROSAUR

Flying reptile

Dinosaur Data

PRONUNCIATION:	TER-OH-**SAW**
SUBORDER:	PTERODACTYLOIDEA
FAMILY:	PTEROSAUR
DESCRIPTION:	FLYING REPTILES
FEATURES:	BIRD-LIKE MEAT EATERS
DIET:	FISH, MOLLUSKS, INSECTS

Pterosaurs were flying reptiles and they lived from the late Triassic period to the end of the Cretaceous period, 228 to 65 million years ago. Pterosaurs were the first vertebrates that were able to fly. When Pterosaurs were first discovered, it was thought that they lived in water. However, in the 19th century Georges Cuvier proposed that pterosaurs flew.

Pterosaur wings were covered with a tough and leathery membrane that stretched between its body, the top of its legs and its fourth finger.

MEGA FACTS

- Pterosaur bones were hollow, just like those of birds.

- Pterosaurs had large brains and good eyesight.

- Some pterosaurs were covered in a type of hair, or fibres.

- Competition with early bird species may have resulted in the extinction of many of the Pterosaurs.

There were many different types of pterosaurs and their wing designs differed. This meant that some of the species flapped their wings and could fly with great power. Others simply glided through the air, relying on updrafts of warm air to help them fly.

Quite a few species of pterosaurs had webbed feet, which could have been used for swimming, but some believe that they were used to help gliding pterosaurs.

When the great extinction wiped out all the dinosaurs at the end of the Cretaceous period, the pterosaurs also disappeared.

199

QUETZALCOATLUS

Feathered serpent god

FLYING DINOSAURS

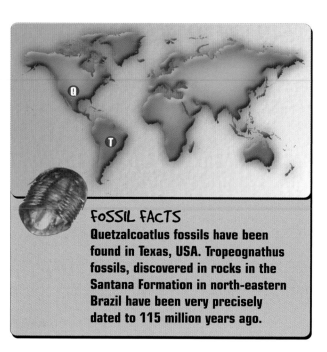

FOSSIL FACTS
Quetzalcoatlus fossils have been found in Texas, USA. Tropeognathus fossils, discovered in rocks in the Santana Formation in north-eastern Brazil have been very precisely dated to 115 million years ago.

Living at the same time as Tyrannosaurus Rex (see page 54) and Triceratops (see page 136) it would have been an impressive sight as it swooped down low over the swampy wetlands of the southern US scavenging for food. Its enormous size made it four times larger than today's scavenging birds, the condors and vultures.

Its outstretched neck was 3 m (10 ft) long with a slim, pointed toothless beak 2 m (6 ft) long. On the top of its head was a short, bony crest. At the front of its wings were small three fingered hands equipped with sharp claws. Swept behind it as it flew were its vast feet – each larger than an adult human's leg.

Quetzalcoatlus was named in 1975 after the Aztec feathered serpent god, although Quetzalcoaltus itself probably didn't have any feathers, just fine fur like a bat.

As with other pterasaurs, and birds today, its hollow bones would have helped it to fly and remain airborne despite its vast size. Using rising thermals to soar through the air, Quetzalcoatlus would have fed on fish or scavenged on rotting carcasses it found around the water's edge.

With a wingspan of 12 m (39 ft), maybe more, it was one of the largest flying animals ever to have lived. It would have weighed around 70 kg (154 lb) – the same sort of weight as an adult human.

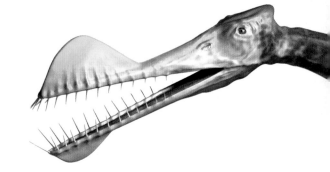

TROPEOGNATHUS

Keel jaw

Dinosaur Data

PRONUNCIATION:	KETT-ZAL-COE-AT-LUSS
SUBORDER:	PTERASAURIA
DESCRIPTION:	LARGE SCAVENGING BIRD
DIET:	FISH, SHELLFISH AND MEAT

With a wingspan of 6 m (20 ft), Tropeognathus was a very large flying reptile.

At 12–14 kg (26–31 lb) it was much lighter than Queztalcoatlus and better suited to preying on fish and squid at the surface of lakes and swamps. It could feed like a flamingo trailing its beak in the water.

For catching, killing and eating it had around 48 teeth in total, 26 slim, pointed teeth in its upper jaw and 22 in the lower one.

Using warm thermals to take off and soar through the air, Tropeognathus would travel many miles in search of food. It tended to remain near water, resting on cliffs as it went but rarely venturing very far inland where it might get hunted.

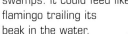

Dinosaur Data

PRONUNCIATION:	TROP-EE-OG-NAY-THUSS
SUBORDER:	PTERASAURIA
DESCRIPTION:	SCAVENGING BIRD
DIET:	FISH AND SQUID

NEW DINOSAUR DISCOVERIES

New dinosaur fossils are being discovered all the time. Here are a few of the most interesting new dinosaurs discovered and named during recent years.

Dilong paradoxus ("paradoxical emperor dragon")

Found: Liaoning Province, China, in 2004
Named: 2004
Period: Lower Cretaceous

This tiny cousin of Tyrannosaurus Rex (see page 54) was covered in primitive hair-like feathers, which probably kept it warm. It was 1.6 m (5 ft) long and weighed around 11 kg (24 lb). Scientists hope that further study of this dinosaur will tell them a lot about the evolution of the tyrannosaurid family. The discovery of a tyrannosaurid with feathers is particularly exciting, because this is the dinosaur family believed to have evolved into birds!

Europasaurus holgeri ("Holger's lizard from Europe")

Found: Northern Germany, in 1998
Named: 2006
Period: Jurassic

This dinosaur was named in June 2006. It belongs to the **sauropod** family. It grew to about the size of a horse, whereas some of its cousins were bigger than buses.

Scientists think it lived on an island. The island could not support larger dinosaurs, so Europasaurus rapidly became smaller, to suit its habitat and food supply.

Microraptor ("little thief")

Found: China, in 1999
Named: 2000
Period: Cretaceous

This **bipedal** carnivore was only about 70 cm (28 in.) long and weighed 1–2 kg (2–4 lb). Its feet were adapted for climbing and it probably lived in trees. It body was thickly covered with feathers, and it had two sets of wings! This may be the most bird-like dinosaur yet found.

Microraptor fossil

Yinlong ("hidden dragon")

Found: Xinjiang Province, China, in 2004
Named: 2006
Period: Late Jurassic

This small herbivore (1.2 m; 4 ft long) is the oldest **ceratopsian** dinosaur ever found, a very early relative of Triceratops (see page 136). It was still small and light enough to walk on its hind legs. Its name comes from the title of the film *Crouching tiger, hidden dragon*, which was filmed close to where its fossils were discovered.

Sauroposeidon
("lizard earthquake God")

Found: Oklahoma, USA in 1994
Named: 1999
Period: Early/Mid Cretaceous

This giant herbivore had longest neck of any dinosaur yet found. It weighed about 60,000 kg (60 tons) and was 18 m (60 ft) tall. It could have raised its head to look in at a six-storey window.

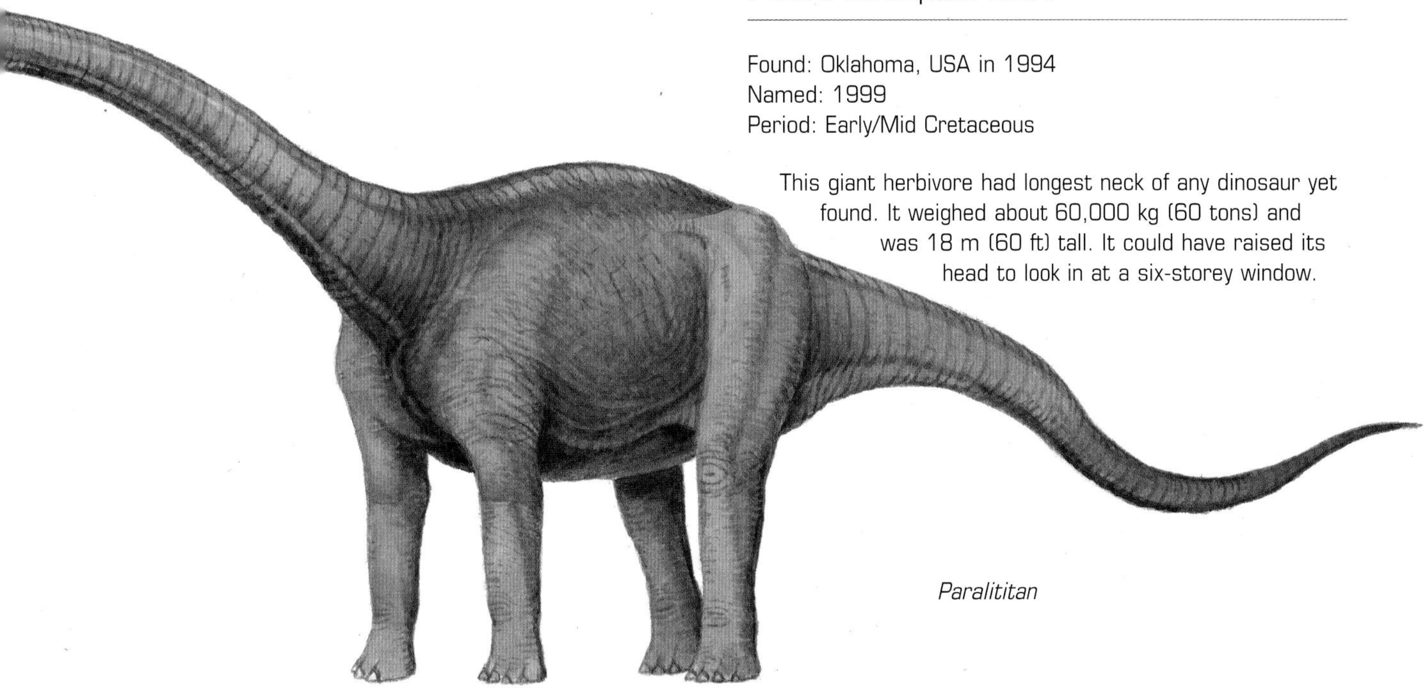

Paralititan

Paralititan ("tidal giant")

Found: Egypt, 2000
Named: 2001
Period: Cretaceous

This giant **herbivore** weighed 50,000 kg (50 tons). It was 27 m (90 ft) long and 9 m (30 ft) tall. Scientists think it may have lived in mangrove swamps.

Mapusaurus roseae
("Earth-lizard from the rose-coloured rocks")

Found: Patagonia, Argentina (South America), in 1997
Named: 2006
Period: Late Cretaceous

At over 12 m (39 ft) long, this huge **carnivore** was bigger than Tyrannosaurus Rex! It weighed over 8,000 kg (8 tons).

It looked much like Tyrannosaurus Rex, but had a longer and narrower skull. Scientists believe it may have hunted in packs that might even have brought down Argentinosaurus (see page 96).

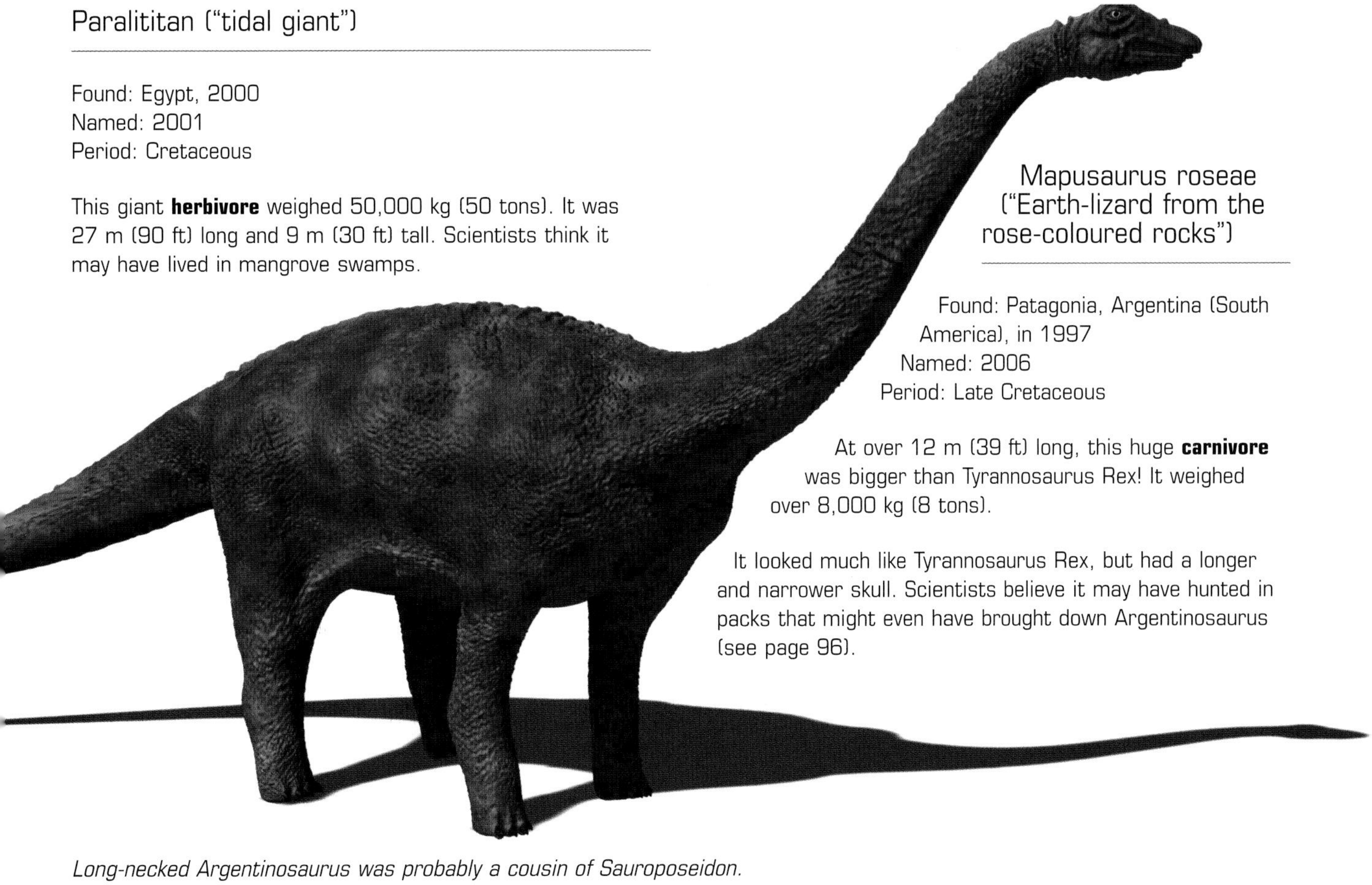

Long-necked Argentinosaurus was probably a cousin of Sauroposeidon.

FOSSIL HUNTING

The only knowledge of dinosaurs comes from fossils. These are often parts of skeletons, but footprints, eggs and occasionally, remains of skin and even droppings have been found.

The discovery of a site can happen by accident, for example, discovering remains while carrying out other work, or alternatively by planned digging with the aim of finding fossils.

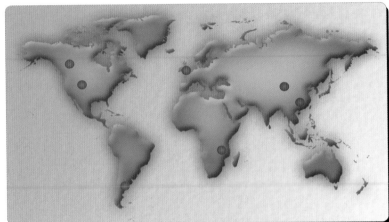

Dinosaurs inhabited all the continents, although at that time the continents were in different places to where they are now. The climates were also quite different. Most fossils are those of sea animals, particularly those that lived in shallow water near the coast, where mud and silt were constantly present to bury their dead remains. As dinosaurs were all land animals, there are very few fossils because their bodies were usually eaten by scavengers or scattered in the wind. If the remains were covered quickly however, a few fossils survived. Sometimes the remains were washed into a nearby stream or river and eventually found their way into a lake or seabed, where they became fossilised.

First fossils

The first dinosaur fossils to be studied scientifically came from western England. The countries where particularly large numbers of dinosaur remains have been found include the United States, Canada, China, Mongolia, Argentina and Tanzania. However, not all of the regions of the world have been investigated fully.

Extraction of fossils

Palaeontologists uncovering a site containing the remains of dinosaurs use techniques that enable them to extract the fossils in the best possible condition. These techniques ensure that we can gather the best possible information about the fossils and prevent any damage during transport to the laboratory to analyse them. There, the fossils are prepared and made available for scientific study and then exhibition to the public.

Having worked out the rough shape of a bone, the surrounding rock needs to be cut away to leave a block. This is then wrapped in a shell of paper and strips of cloth soaked in plaster which, once they have hardened, make it possible to remove the entire block and transport it without breaking or disturbing the fossil inside.

The scientific investigation begins in the field, with a detailed note being made of the position of the bones, in order to record how they are arranged on the site, and the types of rock that surround them.

The remaining surrounding rock is removed using small tools, or dissolved with acid. Once laboratory preparation is complete, each bone is described, measured and analysed in order to identify the animal as precisely as possible and to find out whether it is a new species.

205

WHY DID DINOSAURS DIE OUT?

The dinosaurs lived for more than 150 million years and were the most successful group of animals ever.

They *all* died out 65 million years ago, as did the flying reptiles and most of the sea reptiles. Seventy percent of all species on earth died. This is called **the K-T Extinction Event**.

Most scientists blame a combination of two things:

- a meteorite hitting the Earth (this is called *the impact theory*)
- massive volcanic eruptions.

Impact theory

When the meteorite hit the Earth it made a huge explosion, destroying everything within an area between 400 km (250 miles) and 500 km (312 miles) across. It threw up massive dust clouds that blocked the sunlight, caused huge forest fires, storms and tidal waves. The impact set off a chain reaction of earthquakes and volcanic eruptions. Weather patterns all over the planet changed.

The fires, storms and tidal waves would have killed large numbers instantly. The fires wiped out massive areas of plant life. After the strike, the Earth was surrounding by clouds of dust, shutting out sunlight for about six months. It became very cold, dusty and dark, making it hard for animals to live and breathe. Without sunlight, plant life died. **Herbivores** starved and so did **carnivores** that preyed on them.

The meteorite impact shook the Earth. Deep cracks opened up in the landscape, and earthquakes would have made previously safe areas dangerous to live in.

At the same time as the meteor hit Earth, volcanoes all over the planet erupted – they poured out red-hot lava (liquid rock) that burned everything it touched. Much of the land surface where dinosaurs lived got covered in layers of molten rock. The volcanoes also

Meteorite

Plant eater Sauropod

threw dust and poisonous gases into the air. Some of these were breathed in, others fell back to Earth in acid rain.

Underwater volcanoes erupted, sending water from the sea's bed to the surface. This deep-sea water was low in oxygen and killed most of the plankton living at the surface. The marine reptiles died because some of them fed on the plankton, and others fed on the plankton-eaters.

Other theories

Here are a few of the other theories.

- The climate was cooling. Dinosaurs were unable to adapt to the new conditions.

- Falling sea levels reduced the habitat available to marine and shallow-water dwellers.

- As oceans began to dry up, more land bridges appeared. Dinosaurs could walk across these into new areas looking for food. They came into contact with other dinosaurs, and passed on diseases to which they had no immunity.

- The herbivores ate too much of the Earth's vegetation and so ran out of food. Once the herbivores were gone, the carnivores had nothing to eat and died out too.

- Snakes, lizards, birds and other small animals survived. It is not known why some species survived the K-T Extinction and others did not.

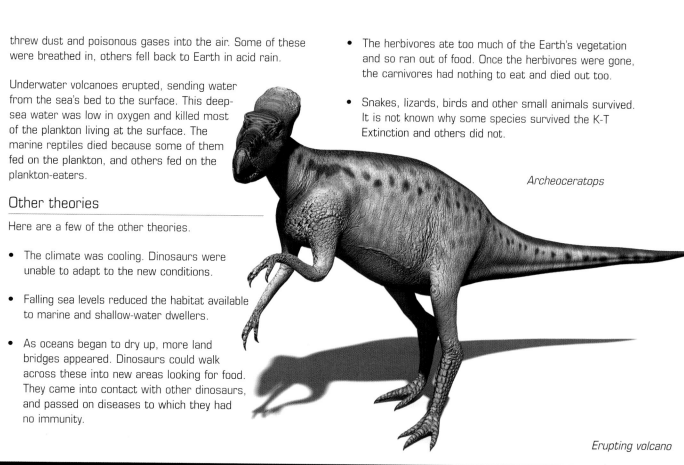

Archeoceratops

Erupting volcano

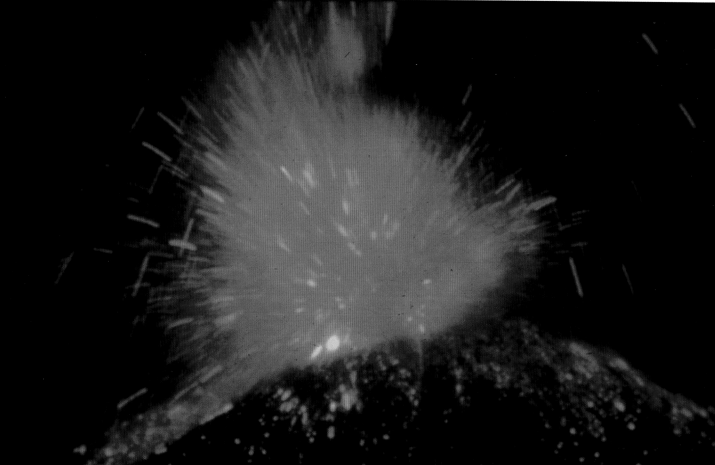

SYNAPSIDS

The sauropsida class includes all reptiles (such as dinosaurs) and, further down the evolutionary scale, all birds as well. The synapsida class contains the pelycosaurs (such as Dimetrodon (see page 16)), the therapsids (ancestors of mammals) and mammals. Mammals are the only surviving synapsids but they are also the dominant land animal on Earth, at least at present, and contained one of the largest known animals – the blue whale.

Pelycosaurs

The very earliest known synapsid is called Archaeothyris. It lived during the Carboniferous period (350 to 300 million years ago) and was one of a group of early synapsids called pelycosaurs that were very successful; they became the dominant land animals in the late Carboniferous and early Permian periods. They were cold-blooded creatures with small brains.

Synapsids are creatures that have a single hole on each side of their skull, where the jaws attach. In the Permian period (300–248 million years ago), there were two types of animals – synapsids, which were the ancient ancestors of mammals, and sauropsids.

208

Therapsids

The therapsids were an advanced group of synapsids that appeared during the first half of the Permian era and by the middle and late Permian era had become the dominant creatures. This group included both **carnivores** and **herbivores** and ranged in size from tiny rat-sized creatures to bulky herbivores weighing as much as 1,000 kg (2,200 lb).

The great extinction

Therapsids remained dominant for millions of years, until a series of massive volcanic eruptions wiped out over 70% of all land dwelling creatures and 90% of all those that dwelt in the vast seas. This was the single most devastating extinction in the entire history of life to date. Though greatly reduced in numbers, a few therapsids did survive into the new Triassic era. However, none of the pelycosaurs survived.

The surviving therapsids were split into three main groups: beaked herbivores called dicynodonts, many of which had a pair of tusk-like teeth (like Lystrosaurus); the cynodonts (see page 210), and finally the therocephalians, a group that did not last beyond the early Triassic period.

Synapsids vs sauropsids

By the early Triassic period, the synapsids were accompanied by sauropsids such as the early archosaurs, some of which were small and lightly built whilst others were as big as, or bigger than, the largest therapsids. Most of these early sauropsids were carnivores whose reptilian metabolism was well suited to the arid and strong monsoon climates of the single great landmass of **Pangaea**, giving them a distinct advantage over the therapsids. So whereas in the Permian period the synapsids had dominated, now it was the turn of the sauropsids.

Dimetrodon

CYNODONTS

Cynodont means 'dog teeth' and is the name given to the direct ancestors of the mammals. These creatures lived during the Triassic and early Jurassic periods at the same time as the archosaurs (the ancestors of the dinosaurs).

Teeth and jaws

The cynodonts had teeth that had many points rather than just one. This meant that they could have much more specialised diets. The teeth of the lower and upper jaw met over a broad area when the mouth was closed, so they were able to grind and chew food more efficiently.

As well as having different types of teeth, the jaw of the cynodonts had a reduced number of jaw bones compared to the earlier synapsids. The 'spare' bones became parts of the mammal's inner ear. Improved hearing gave these creatures a better awareness of their environment – a definite advantage – this also meant that they needed to be able to process more information in their brains, leading to larger brains.

Evolution

Cynodonts also developed a secondary palate in the roof of the mouth. This allowed air to flow to the lungs through the back of the mouth, allowing cynodonts to chew and breathe at the same time. This characteristic is present in all mammals today except adult humans.

Unlike the dicynodonts, which remained large, the cynodonts became progressively smaller and more mammal-like as time went on. The largest cynodonts were roughly the size of a wolf and were much smaller than the archosaurs that were around at the same time.

Whether through changing climate, changing vegetation, competition from other creatures, or a combination of factors, most of the large cynodonts and dicynodonts had disappeared before the Jurassic era. Their places were taken by the archosaur's descendants – the dinosaurs. The cynodonts that survived were smaller and evolved into the earliest mammals.

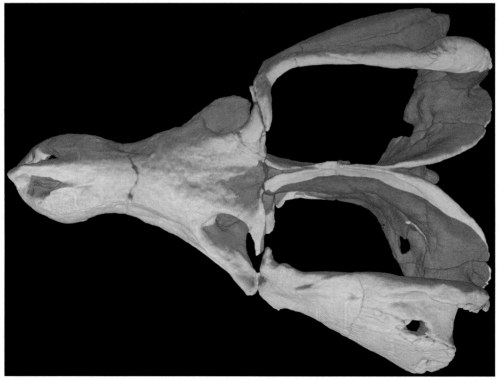

Cynodont skull

Cynognathus (sy-nog-NAY-thus)

This wolf-sized cynodont lived in the mid-Triassic period, about 245–230 million years ago. It was a swift carnivorous quadruped with powerful jaws sporting a wide variety of teeth – sharp incisors, long canines and shearing cheek teeth. It was a pack hunter, its principal prey being herbivorous therapsids such as Kannemeyeria.

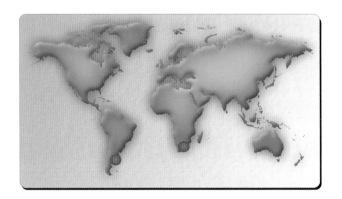

Cynognathus was roughly 1.5 m (5 ft) long, was probably warm-blooded and may have been hairy – although we cannot know this for certain as soft-tissues 'like hair' do not survive fossilisation.

It's name means 'dog jaw' and was given by H.G. Seeley in 1876. Fossils have been found in Argentina and South Africa.

Fossilised head of Cynognathus crateronotus

EARLY MAMMALS

The earliest mammals evolved in the Triassic period alongside the archosaurs, after the great extinction that marked the end of the Permian period.

Mammals evolved from the cynodonts (see page 210). Like other synapsids they have only one hole in their skull where the jaw muscles attach. However, unlike other synapsids they have mammary glands – organs that in the females of the species produce milk for the young. This feature is unique to mammals.

Mammals possess another unique feature, a section of the brain called the neo-cortex. This is associated with the senses, movement and awareness of space and, in humans, language and thought.

The very first mammal is widely accepted to have been Megazostrodon, a sleek, tiny **quadruped** with a long tail and long snout. This little creature probably ate insects, measured about 10 cm (4 in.) long and weighed about 200 g (8 oz). A complete fossilised skeleton was found in Lesotho (in South Africa).

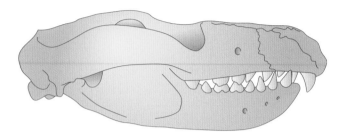

Most of the early mammals were small, shrew-like nocturnal scurrying creatures that lived primarily by hunting insects. In 2000 fossils of a mammal named Repenomamus measuring approximately 1 m (3 ft) long were found in China.

A mammal fossil was found in China, with the fossilised remains of a small dinosaur in its stomach (a young Psitticasosaurus (see page 152)), indicating that larger mammals preyed on dinosaurs! This dramatically altered the view of how early mammals coexisted with the dinosaurs.

However, even the larger specimens of mammals were in the shadow of the dinosaurs until the dinosaurs became extinct.

Megalostrodon fossil

Monotremes

Whilst they survived the cataclysmic impact that ended the age of the dinosaurs, the multituberculata became extinct about 34 million years ago (roughly 30 million years after the dinosaurs).

Monotremes ('single opening') have several features that distinguish them from other mammals. Firstly their reproductive, urinary and anal tracts all open into a single duct (called the cloaca), this feature is the one that gave rise to their name; secondly they lay eggs rather than give birth to live young and, whilst they have mammary glands, they have no nipples – milk for the newly hatched young is instead secreted from the skin along their underbellies.

There were once many kinds of monotremes but only two survive – the duck-billed platypus and the spiny anteater (also known as Echidna). Both these families are now only native to Australia and New Guinea, although in 1991 a fossilised tooth from a monotreme was found in Argentina.

Multituberculata

This mammal subclass first appeared during the middle of the Jurassic period. They were small and rodentlike. They were distinguished by their teeth, which had multiple points arranged in rows, these points are also sometimes referred to as "tubercles", hence multituberculata or "many points."

The bat is the only mammal that can truly fly, rather than simply glide.

MARSUPIALS

There are around 330 species of marsupials today. Probably the best-known marsupial is the kangaroo.

The earliest fossil of a marsupial yet discovered was found in China in 2003 and belongs to a species called Sinodelphys szalayi. This little creature was about the size of a chipmunk, being 15 cm (6 in.) long from nose to tail and weighed only about 30 g (1 oz). It probably spent most of its time scampering through the branches of trees as it hunted worms, grubs and other insects. This ability to climb would also have helped it evade predators.

The largest marsupial ever to have existed is Diprotodon, at 1.7 m (5 ft) tall, and weighing up to 2,500 kg (5,000 lb). It was a **quadruped** and an **herbivore**. The strong claws on its front may have allowed it to dig up roots to supplement its grazing. Several fossilised footprints have been found. These still bear the impressions of fur so we know that Diprotodon was definitely a furry giant!

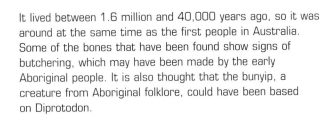

It lived between 1.6 million and 40,000 years ago, so it was around at the same time as the first people in Australia. Some of the bones that have been found show signs of butchering, which may have been made by the early Aboriginal people. It is also thought that the bunyip, a creature from Aboriginal folklore, could have been based on Diprotodon.

Thylacoleo Carnifex

Thylacoleo Carnifex, the 'marsupial lion' lived from about 24 million years ago right up until 50,000 years ago (the end of the last Ice Age). It was a quadruped, about 1.5 m (5 ft) long and may have weighed over 200 kg (440 lb). It had very strong forelimbs and retractable claws. Scientists believe it could climb trees, perhaps dragging prey up there to eat in safety.

The marsupial lion's teeth and jaw were really special. It had very large incisors (sharp teeth for tearing into meat) and calculations show that it would have had the strongest bite of any mammal species, extinct or living. A 100 kg (220 lb) marsupial lion's bite would have been stronger than that of a 250 kg (550 lb) African lion.

This impressive beast is very similar to a mythical creature called the dropbear from Australian Aboriginal folklore — this creature used to lurk in trees and drop upon unwary travellers!

Thylacinus

The last marsupial carnivore to have existed is Thylacinus, also known as the marsupial wolf or Tasmanian tiger. This animal was about the size of a tiger and a cunning predator, though unlike the wolf it hunted alone. It could open its jaws further than any other mammal!

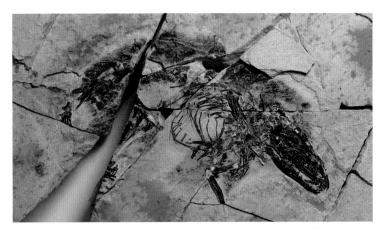

Sinodelphys szalayi fossil

Dinosaur tracks

Thylacinus was common in Tasmania in the 19th century, but its numbers were greatly reduced in the late 19th and early 20th century and it is now thought to be extinct. The last known Thylacinus died in captivity in 1936. However, scientists have recently been investigating the possibility of cloning a Thylacinus from preserved samples.

PLACENTALS

Placentals are now the dominant subclass of mammals. There are almost 4,000 different species of them – including mice, cats, dogs, whales, dolphins and humans. The name placentals refers to the placenta, an organ in the female that forms the connection between the mother and the foetus and helps to nourish the foetus and filter waste.

Eomaia scansoria

The first placental mammal is widely believed to be Eomaia scansoria ('climbing dawn mother'). Its fossil was found in Yixin in China in 2000 and is approximately 125 million years old, indicating that it lived in the early Cretaceous period when the dinosaurs dominated the planet.

Like the majority of early mammals, it was a small rodent-like creature, about 10 cm (4 in.) long and weighing 20–25 g (1 oz). Tiny details are visible, including the tiny bones of its feet and even its fur!

Some scientists have recently disputed whether Eomaia was a true placental mammal, suggesting it may instead have been one of the immediate ancestors of this line instead.

Whales

The largest placental mammal ever to have existed is the blue whale. The largest recorded specimen was 33.5 m (109 ft) long and weighed 190,000 kg (190 tons)! The blue whale is also the loudest creature recorded – its call could be heard underwater for hundreds of miles and reach up to 188 decibels, which is louder than a jet engine! Whales are the only mammals that have evolved to live in the open ocean and one of only two mammals that spend their entire lives in water (the other is the manatee or sea cow).

Two fossils of Eomaia scansoria

Dolphin

Fossil records show that whales evolved from hoofed mammals, who adapted to return to the ocean. The oldest whale fossil known, of *Himalayecetus subathuensis*, is 53.5 million years old and was found in the foothills of the Himalayan mountain range in India (an area which was underwater at that time!). This primitive whale was about 3 m (10 ft) long and had functional legs, indicating it may have spent some of its time on land.

Andrewsarchus

The largest land-based carnivorous placental mammal is thought to have been Andrewsarchus. This heavily built wolf-like predator roamed the world from 60 million years ago to roughly 32 million years ago. It was about 4–5m (13–16 ft) long and weighed up to 2,000 kg (2 tons)! Its huge 1 m (3ft) skull contained large sharp teeth for tearing meat, and flatter cheek teeth that may have

been used for crushing bones. Unlike the wolf which it is thought to have resembled, Andrewsarchus had hoofed feet. It is believed it may have been an ancestor of the whales. The first fossil of this creature was found in Mongolia in 1923 by Kan Chen Pao and was named after Roy Chapman Andrews, the palaeontologist who led the expedition.

EARLY CARNIVORES

The order of mammals called the 'carnivora' evolved about 55 million years ago (roughly 10 million years after the extinction of the dinosaurs) and eventually gave rise to the canine and feline predators like wolves and lions.

Carnivora have enlarged canine teeth (the sharp single-pointed teeth at the front of the jaw, near the middle) and one pair of the molars (the teeth at the back of the jaw) are sharp and bladelike, coming together in a scissor like action when the jaw shuts. Both types of teeth are adaptations that are very useful for tearing and slicing meat.

Creodonts

Initially, the dominant carnivores were a group of mammals called the Creodonts. Creodonts remained the dominant carnivores until about 30 million years ago, when they began to decline. One possible reason for this is competition with the carnivora, who had larger brains and a more efficient method of running.

Carnivora

The earliest carnivora belonged to a group called *Miacids*, small creatures rather like modern pine-martens, with long bodies, short legs and long tails. Their paws were wide with the toes spread quite far apart and the first digit opposed to the others (like a human thumb is opposed to the fingers). They would have been good climbers, especially with their long tails to use for balance. These early carnivores primarily ate lizards, birds and smaller shrew-like mammals as well as invertebrates.

Mongoose

Caniforms and feliforms

These earliest carnivores evolved into two distinct families, the caniforms and the feliforms. The caniforms were dog-like carnivores that gave rise to dogs, bears, raccoons and martens. The feliforms were the cat-like carnivores and gave rise to cats, hyenas and mongeese.

Sabre-tooths

Perhaps the most famous of the prehistoric carnivores is the sabre-toothed cat. These creatures were powerful feliform carnivores with long wickedly sharp canine teeth, which could be well over 10 cm (4 in.) long!

Probably the best known sabre-tooth is Smilodon. This awe-inspiring predator evolved around 2 million years ago and survived until about 10,000 years ago. It was about 1.5 m (5 ft) long, 1 m (3 ft) tall and weighed over 200 kg (440 lb), with canine teeth 18 cm (7 in.) long! It was adept at springing onto prey but was a fairly slow runner. This has lead some scientists to speculate that it hunted in packs – some members of the pack would startle prey and drive them out so other members could catch and kill them. Other evidence to support this idea comes from fossils of Smilodons that had recovered from quite severe wounds. As they would have been unable to hunt their own prey whilst they were healing, some scientists have suggested that they instead fed on the leftovers from kills made by the other members of the pack.

There were many species of sabre-tooths, not all of whom were cats. One example is Thylacosmilus, which lived 3 million years ago. It had huge canine teeth but it was a marsupial and so more closely related to the kangaroo than the cat family.

Skeleton of Smilodon

FICTIONAL DINOSAURS

Dinosaurs in books

A popular theme in stories featuring dinosaurs is the discovery of a 'lost world' where dinosaurs still roam.

Journey to the Centre of the Earth is a science-fiction story written by Jules Verne, and published in 1864. It tells the story of an eccentric professor who leads his nephew and a hired guide to the 'centre of the Earth'. Here they find a whole world of danger, including many prehistoric animals – they are almost eaten by an ichthyosaur, which they observe fighting and killing a plesiosaur.

The Lost World was written by Sir Arthur Conan-Doyle and published in 1912. The eccentric Professor Challenger leads a party of adventurers on an expedition to a mysterious plateau in the Amazon, where dinosaurs still survive. Among the dinosaurs they discover are pterodactyls, one of which they capture and take back to England. There it escapes, leaving the adventurers unable to prove their story!

Michael Crichton's novel *Jurassic Park* and its sequel *The Lost World* featured dinosaurs that had been created by scientists from fossilised genetic material of the extinct creatures, and put into an island theme park.

Dinosaurs are a popular choice for children's books. In the 'Harry and His Bucketful of Dinosaurs' series, Harry jumps into his bucket of toy dinosaurs and is magically transported to 'Dino World', where his toys are now full-sized living dinosaurs.

Dinosaurs on the big screen

Gertie the Dinosaur made her debut in 1914. A cartoonist called Winsor McCay makes a bet with some of his artist friends that he can bring a dinosaur to life. He draws Gertie, and when she comes to life Winsor steps into the cartoon and joins her. A model of Gertie can be seen beside a lake at Disneyland in Florida.

The Lost World was first turned into a film in 1925. This film has been remade four times.

The characters in *King Kong,* a film made in 1933, encountered a fierce Stegosaurus and a meat-eating Apatosaurus. In reality both these dinosaurs were plant-eaters! Kong also battles a Tyrannosaurus Rex, defeating it and going on to fight both a pterosaur and a plesiosaur.

Various dinosaurs featured in the animated Walt Disney film *Fantasia* in 1940; the dinosaurs appeared in the musical sequence *The Rite of Spring*.

Dinosaur was a feature film released in 2000. It was made by Walt Disney Pictures, combining real backgrounds with computer-animated dinosaurs. It follows the adventures of a young Iguanodon, Aladar, as he travels with a herd of peaceful dinosaurs toward their traditional nesting ground. Aladar and some of the weaker dinosaurs – a Brachiosaurus, a Styracosaurus and an Ankylosaurus – are left behind by the herd, but save the day when the herd is attacked by the vicious predator Carnotaurus.

Jurassic Park and its sequels brought dinosaurs to the big screen in realistic detail. The films use the recreation of extinct dinosaurs to give us an exciting adventure story, and also to warn about the dangers that greed and the irresponsible use of science can create.

A famous screen dinosaur is Rex, the green toy dinosaur from the films *Toy Story 1* and *2* – a shy dinosaur who was always afraid that he wasn't being 'scary enough'.

Cartoon dinosaurs

Dino appeared in *The Flintstones*, an American cartoon series that became one of the most successful TV cartoon series ever. Dino was the dinosaur pet of the Flintstones, a prehistoric family of cavemen. He behaved much like a pet dog. The Flintstones – and Dino – have appeared in two movies, *The Flintstones* (1994) and *The Flintstones in Viva Rock Vegas* (2000).

The animated film *The Land Before Time* and its eleven sequels feature the adventures of an orphaned Apatosaurus called Littlefoot. His friends are other young dinosaurs:

- *Cera*, a tough and bossy female Triceratops

- *Ducky*, a sweet, loyal female Saurolophus

- *Petrie*, a Pterodactyl who is afraid of flying

- *Spike*, an ever-hungry Stegosaurus.

The gang of friends have many adventures, and learn much about life, all the while avoiding the dreaded 'sharpteeth' (carnivores).

FICTIONAL DINOSAURS

Dinosaurs on television

In the early 1990s, dinosaurs even got their own soap opera! *Dinosaurs* was a live-action comedy with humans inside dinosaur costumes, their voices provided by actors. The show featured a family of 'civilised dinosaurs', the Sinclairs, who faced many of the same issues as people. All the members of the family were different dinosaurs – the father, Earl, was a Megalosaurus, while his wife, Fran, appeared to be an Allosaurus.

In 1974, the science-fiction series *Doctor Who* had a story *Invasion of the dinosaurs* in which prehistoric dinosaurs were brought to London by a time machine.

Dinosaurs in computer games

Dinosaurs feature in video games. Here are just some of them.

- **Prince Tricky** in the *Star Fox* universe. Tricky is a Triceratops.

- In the **Dino Crisis** series, players battled dinosaurs from the past.

- In **Dino Stalker,** the hero was a World War II pilot who was shot down and regained consciousness in prehistoric times.

- **Greymon** and **MetalGreymon** are characters in the monster game and cartoon series *Digimon*.

Dinosaur 'celebrities'

Here are two dinosaur 'celebrities'.

Barney
Barney and friends is a TV show. Barney, a purple dinosaur who looks vaguely like a tyrannosaur, helps young children to

learn through songs and games. Barney was created in 1987, and *Barney and friends* was first shown in 1992.

Godzilla

Godzilla was a radioactive prehistoric monster who attacked Tokyo and other Japanese cities in a series of films. Godzilla was subjected to nuclear radiation and, as a result, grew to giant size and gained unusual powers. Godzilla has appeared in more than 28 Japanese films. Godzilla also appeared in less villainous form in his own cartoon series, gaining the younger and smaller companion Godzuki. In 1998, a new film was made by TriStar Pictures, set in modern day New York.

DRAGONS

Komodo dragon

were said to wrap their victims in their coils and crushed them to death – just like a large constrictor snake.

Over time, these – and possibly other – elements all came together to give us what we think of as dragons – fearsome lizard-like monsters with wings, who could breathe fire. They were thought to guard great hoards of treasure and are often used in stories to symbolise greed.

The closest thing to a living dragon now is the komodo dragon from the East Indies. This is a great monitor lizard and is the largest living lizard in the world, 2–3 m (6–9 ft) long, equipped with sharp teeth and long, powerful claws. Komodo dragons are effective hunters – they have even on rare occasions been known to kill people.

Many people think that the discovery of huge fossilised bones from creatures that must have looked like huge lizards helped to create the myth of dragons.

In the West, dragons have always been considered evil and monstrous, whereas in the East, especially in China, they are revered as wise and powerful.

Dragons do have other traits that are hard to explain just by the discovery of dinosaur bones. For example, it is almost compulsory for Western dragons to breathe fire. It may be that the sight of fiery meteorites and comets in the ancient night sky gave birth to the idea of flying, fire-breathing monsters – comets were often referred to in medieval times as 'dragon stars'.

Most of the earliest dragons are described as legless. The word dragon comes from the Latin word *draco* (snake). These giant monsters

Viking boat prow showing dragon head

DRAGON DATA

- The red dragon is the national symbol of Wales. Probably the most famous dragon in Britain, it is called Y Draig Goch in Welsh. Dragons appear in many tales of Celtic mythology. In the *Mabinogion* a red dragon fights a white dragon which is trying to invade Britain. The fighting dragons create a terrifying noise and King Lludd lures them to fall into a pit full of mead. They drink the alcoholic mead and fall asleep. Legend has it they are still there, imprisoned under Snowdonia, the highest mountain in Wales.

- A dragon named Tiamat features in the Babylonian creation myth – she was slain by the greatest hero of the gods, Marduk, who split her body in two and used half of it to create the Earth and the other half to create the sky.

- St George, the patron saint of England, is famous for slaying a dragon. This did not take place in England, however, but in far-off Syria!

- Dragons feature in the oldest known epic tale – the *Epic of Gilgamesh* from around 3000 BC.

- Raiding Vikings carved fierce dragon heads on the prows of their longboats to strike terror into the hearts of their enemies.

- The constellation of *Draco* – the Dragon – is found between the Great Bear (the Plough) and the Little Bear.

- In medieval times, dishonest people wishing to make money from displaying 'marvels' faked the remains of 'baby dragons' using lizard bodies and the wings of bats.

- The 17th century English term *dragoon* for soldiers that had horses but dismounted to fight on foot, came from the 'fire-spitting' wide-bore muskets that they used. (A musket is a very primitive form of gun.)

CHINESE DRAGONS

The oldest dragon stories come from China. Eastern dragons have usually been considered benevolent (kind). They look different too – they do not usually have wings, and have a snake-like body, several clawed feet like those of an eagle, feathery manes and huge eyes. They are often shown holding a magic pearl that allows them to control lightning. They also have horns like a stag.

Chinese dragons were believed to have control over the elements, and so the weather. They brought the vital rains, and commanded all areas of water – lakes, seas, rivers and oceans. They are associated with wisdom, and long life.

Eastern dragons probably originated as tribal animal totems, which depicted animals in a highly stylised way, and often combined the attributes and body parts of various creatures.

Dragons evolved from this to be seen as mythical creatures. They were said to have the power to change shape.

Dragons were strongly associated with water and there were thought to be four major Dragon Kings who represented the Seas of the East, West, North and South.

Dragons were portrayed in art and decoration in different ways, using a kind of code: a dragon embroidered onto silk with five claws meant a king; four claws were for a prince; and just three meant a lesser courtier.

The dragon was a symbol of imperial authority for many Chinese dynasties. The legendary First Emperor, the Huang Di (the Yellow Emperor) used the symbol, and was said to have turned into a dragon when he died and ascended to heaven. The imperial throne was named the Dragon Throne. Because he was the first Emperor, there is an old folk custom of the Chinese people referring to themselves as 'children of the dragon'.

DRAGON DATA

- The Mandarin Chinese word for dragon is 'leong'.

- One of the 12 signs of the Chinese Zodiac is the Dragon. People born in the years of the Dragon are said to be honest, brave, healthy, energetic and generous.

- There is a Chinese proverb that runs 'hoping one's child will become a dragon' – this means, they hope the child will grow up to be as powerful and successful as a dragon.

- In Chinese myth, dragons are associated with good luck.

Today, dragons feature heavily in Chinese celebrations all over the world. At special festivals, such as Chinese New Year, 'dragon boat races' are held. These boats have magnificent carved dragons at the prow, and are rowed by up to 12 people. 'Dragon dancing' can also be seen on festive occasions – large wood-and-cloth dragons, with masks for heads and long bodies, are given life by people who support the dragon with poles and dance it through the streets. These 'dragon dancers' need to be very fit and well-trained.

THE LOCH NESS MONSTER

Loch Ness, in the highlands of Scotland, is a huge lake to have to search – it is 36.8 km (22.8 miles) long and nearly 1.5 km (1 mile) wide. It is also an impressive 137 m (450 ft) deep, plunging to almost 305 m (1,000 ft) in places.

Some people believe that there is a monster in the murky waters of Loch Ness. There have been many reported sightings, but there is still no evidence that the creature exists. Even attempts to find it by searching the entire lake with sonar have failed, though they have produced findings of large objects that cannot be identified. Attempts to find the 'monster' are still being made.

The Life of Saint Columba from the 6th century tells a story of the saint rescuing an unfortunate local from a monster in the River Ness and ordering it into the depths of the lake.

Descriptions

The first alleged modern sighting of the creature was in 1933, and it was then that newspapers first coined the

phrase 'Loch Ness Monster'. Since then people have claimed to see the 'monster' on more than 1,000 occasions. Most of the descriptions share some or all of the following characteristics:

- a serpent-like neck or body
- a snake-like or a horse-like head
- v-shaped ripples in the water
- gaping mouth
- horns or antennae on top of the head
- dark grey colour (like an elephant)
- many accounts describe an animal 'rolling' or 'plunging' in the water.

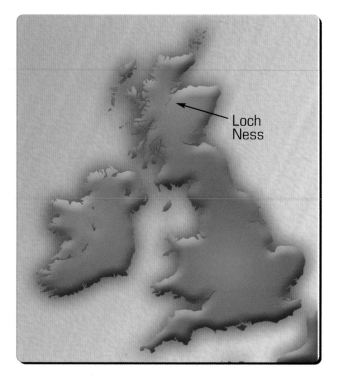

Loch Ness

Theories

Most scientists believe these accounts describe an animal most like an extinct dinosaur – a plesiosaur. Plesiosaurs lived from the late Triassic to the Cretaceous period. The similarity between them and descriptions of the Loch Ness Monster has led some to suggest that a whole breeding colony of plesiosaurs has survived, possibly hidden in caverns beneath the lake. Such a huge underwater cavern was discovered by coastguard George Edwards in 1989.

Many biologists say that Loch Ness could not support even a tiny group of such creatures, even if the idea of them surviving for such a length of time were likely.

Other people suggest that a breeding colony of plesiosaurs has survived out in the ocean – and that sometimes babies swim into the loch and grow too big to get out.

Evidence

In 2003, fossil plesiosaur bones were actually found in Loch Ness. However, the scientists who examined them found that the four vertebrae had been brought from elsewhere and planted deliberately.

Most surface photographs of the monster are unclear, and the most famous picture, the 'surgeon's photograph' from the 1930s, has been admitted to be a fake.

In the 1970s, a research group obtained some underwater photographs after scouring the loch with sonar. These pictures seem to show a roughly plesiosaur-shaped creature, in particular close ups of a diamond-shaped 'fin'. People still do not agree whether they show a moving fin or simply bubble patterns in the water.

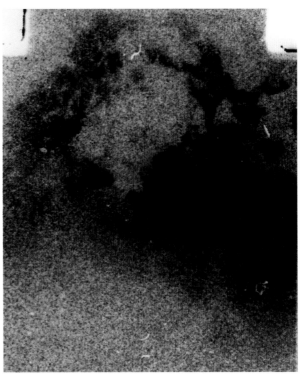

Sonar image of Nessie

PRONUNCIATION GUIDE

A

Acrocanthosaurus	ak-row-KAN-tho-SAWR-us
Allosaurus	AL-uh-SAWR-us
Altirhinus	All-tee-ryne-us
Ankylosaurus	ANG-ki-lo-SAWR-us
Apatosaurus	a-PAT-oh-SAWR-us
Arrhinoceratops	Ay-rye-no-serra-tops
Archaeopteryx	ark-eeOP-ter-iks
Argentinosaurus	ahy-gen-TEEN-oh-SAWR-us

B

Baronyx	BAR-ee-ON-iks
Brachiosaurus	brack-ee-oh-SAWR-us

C

Camarasurus	kuh-MARE-uh-SAWR-us
Camptosaurus	kamp-toe-SAWR-us
Carcharodontosaurus	Kar-kar-owe-don-toe-SAWR-us
Carnotaurus	KAR-no-TAWR-us
Caudipteryx	caw-DIP-ter-iks
Centrosaurus	SEN-tro-SAWR-us
Coelophysis	see-law-FYS-iss
Coelurus	seel-yur-us

Compsognathus — komp-so-NATH-us
Corythosaurus — cor-IH-thoh-SAWR-us

D

Deinonychus	dyn-ON-ik-us
Dimetrodon	die-MET-roe-don
Dimorphodon	die-MORF-oh-don
Diplodocus	dip-LOD-oh-kus
Drinker	DRINK-er
Dromaeosaurus	DROH-mee-oh-SAWR-us
Dryosaurus	dry-owe-SAWR-us

E

Edaphosaurus	ah-DAF-oh-SAW-us
Edmontonia	ed-mon-TONE-ee-ah
Edmontosaurus	ed-MON-toe-SAWR-us
Elasmosaurus	ee-LAZ-moh-sawr-us
Eoraptor	EE-oh-RAP-tor
Eryops	AR-ee-ops

G

Gallimimus	GALL-ih-MIME-us
Gerrothorax	geh-roh-THOR-ax
Gigantosaurus	Jig-a-NOT-oh-SAWR-us
Gryposaurus	grip-owe-SAWr-us

H

Hadrosaurus	HAD-row-SAWR-us
Herrerasaurus	he-ray-raar-SAWR-us
Hesperornis	HES-per-OR-nis
Huayangosaurus	hoo-ah-yang-oh-SAWR-us
Hypacrosaurus	high-pah-kroe-SAWR-us
Hypsilophodon	hip-sill-owe-foe-don

I

Ichthyosaurus	IK-thee-oh-SAWR-us
Iguanodon	ig-WAN-oh-DON

K

Kentrosaurus	KEN-troh-SAWR-us
Kronosaurus	crow-no-sawr-us

L

Leaellynasaura	lee-ell-lin-ah-SAWR-ah

Leptoceratops   lep-toe-SERR-a-tops
Liopleurodon   LIE-oh-PLOO-ro-don

M

Maiasaura   MY-ah-SAWR-ah
Megalosaurus   MEG-uh-low-SAWR-us
Melanosaurus   mel-uh-NOR-uh-SAWR-us
Microceratops   my-kro-SAYR-ah-tops
Minmi   MIN-mee
Mosasaurus   MOES-ah-SAWR-us

N

Nodosaurus   noh-doh-SAWR-us
Nothosaurus   no-tho-SAWR-us

O

Opthamosaurus   off-THAL-moh-SAW-rus
Orodromeus   orrow-drom-ee-us
Othnielia   oth-nigh-ell-ee-ah
Oviraptor   o-vih-RAP-tor

P

Panoplosaurus   pan-oh-ploh-SAWR-us
Parasaurolophus   par-ah-SAWR-oh-LOW-fuss
Piatnizkysaurus   Pee-at-nits-key-SAWR-us
Plesiosaurus   PLEE-see-o-SAWR-us
Procomsognathus   pro-comp-son-ay-thus
Protoceratops   pro-toe-SERR-a-tops
Psittacosaurus   SIT-ah-koe-SAWR-us
Pteranodon   ter-an-owe-don
Pterosaur   ter-oh-SAW

Q

Quetzalcoatlus   kett-zal-coe-at-lus

R

Rhamphorhynchus   RAM-for-INK-us

S

Saltasaurus   salt-ah-SAWR-us
Saltopus   sall-toe-pus
Saurornithoides   SAWR-or-nih-THOY-deez
Scelidosaurus   skel-ee-doh-SAWR-us
Scutellosaurus   sku-TEL-oh-SAWR-us

Seismosaurus   size-moh-SAWR-us
Shonisaurus   SHON-e-SAWR-us
Spinosaurus   SPINE-o-SAWR-us
Stegosaurus   STEG-oh-SAWR-us
Stygimoloch   STIG-ih-MOE-lock
Styracosaurus   sty-rack-oh-SAWR-us

T

Tenontosaurus   ten-on-toe-SAWR-us
Thescelosaurus   thess-kell-owe-SAWR-us
Titanosaurus   tie-TAN-oh-SAWR-us
Triceratops   try-SER-a tops
Troodon   TRUE-oh-don
Tropeognathus   trop-ee-og-nay-thus
Tylosaurus   TIE-low-SAWR-us
Tyrannosaurus   TIE-ran-owe-SAWR-us

U

Ultrasaurus   ULL-tra-SAWR-us

V

Velociraptor   vuh-LOSS-ih-RAP-tor

GLOSSARY

ammonite extinct marine molluscs, had coiled shells

ancestor animal from which a later, related animal has evolved

ankylosaurs a group of armoured herbivores that lived 76–68 million years ago. There were three main groups of ankylosaurs – ankylosaurids (like Ankylosaurus, see p118–119), polacanthids and nodosaurids 'node lizard' (nodosaurids differed from the other two types of ankylosaur that they had spines sticking outward from their shoulders and neck)

aquatic water-dwelling

archosaurs triassic reptiles, immediate ancestors of the dinosaurs

binocular vision ability to focus on the same thing with two eyes

biped animal that walks on two hind legs

bipedal walks on two legs

bonebed site where many fossils from the same time period have been found

browsing feeding on high-up leaves, trees and shrubs

camouflage colouring allowing an animal to blend in with its surroundings

canine teeth pointed cone-shaped teeth

carnivore a meat eater

carrion dead body (eaten by scavengers)

ceratopsian plant-eating dinosaurs with horned faces

coelurosaurs 'hollow-tail lizards' – early members of this group were very small, but its members in the end included the most likely ancestors of modern birds

cold-blooded cold-blooded creatures rely on their environment to regulate their body temperature

conifer evergreen trees and shrubs

cretaceous last period of the Mesozoic era, 135–65 million years ago

cycad plant like a palm tree with a middle trunk and leaves

descendent animal whose evolution can be traced back to a particular animal or group

dinosaurs land-dwelling reptiles from the Mesozoic era

erosion the wearing away of the Earth's surface by natural forces

evolution process by which one species changes into another, usually over a long period of time

extinction the dying out of an entire species

extinction-level event catastrophe resulting in the extinction of many species at once (mass extinction)

femur main thigh bone

fenestrae gap or holes in bone, from the Latin for windows

fern leafy plant growing in damp places

fibula calf bone

fossil remains preserved in rock

geologist person who studies rock

gingko primitive seed-bearing tree with fan shaped leaves, common in Mesozoic era

grazing feeding on low-growing plants

hadrosaurs duck-billed plant-eating dinosaurs

herbivore an animal which just eats plants

horsetail primitive spore-bearing plant, common in Mesozoic era

ichthyosaurs sea-dwelling prehistoric reptiles

incisor tooth adapted for cutting and gnawing, usually at the front of the mouth

incubate maintain eggs at good temperature for growth and development

invertebrate animal which has no backbone

jurassic period of the Mesozoic era, 203–135 million years ago

Jurassic Coast area of the coast near Lyme Regis in England, where Mary Anning found many of the fossils that made her famous

juvenile young – not yet an adult

K-T Extinction Event extinction event which occurred at the end of the Cretaceous period resulting in extinction of the dinosaurs and many other species

Lesothaurus Triassic dinosaur

lizard scaly-bodied, air breathing reptile with backbone that evolved from amphibians

mammal hairy warm-blooded animal that nourishes young from mammary glands and evolved during Triassic period

marsupial mammals that give birth to young which then develop in mother's pouch

membrane thin layer of tissue protecting embryo in egg

Mesozoic era age of reptiles, 248–65 million years ago which includes Triassic, Jurassic and Cretaceous periods

molars teeth designed for grinding food

mosasaurs types of marine reptiles

omnivore animal which eats a mixed diet of plants and meat

ornithopods beaked, usually bipedal, plant-eating dinosaurs that flourished from the late Triassic to the late Cretaceous (ornithopod means bird feet)

orthacanthus a primitive shark

ossicles pea-sized bones

palaeontologist person who studies fossils

Pangaea the 'super-continent' formed of all Earth's land masses

paravertebrae extra bony plates added to backbone of dinosaur

plesiosaurs large marine reptiles that lived in Mesozoic era (not dinosaurs)

predator animal which hunts other animals to eat

premolars teeth behind the canines and in front of the molars

primates group of mammals, including monkeys, humans and their ancestors

primitive basic, at an early stage of development

pterandons a group of flying reptiles that were usually toothless and had a short tail

pterodophytes a type of fern (a plant)

pterosaurs flying prehistoric reptiles (not dinosaurs but lived at the same time)

quadruped animal that walks on all fours

rhynchorsaurs herbivorous reptiles from Mezozoic era

sauropods giant, plant-eating dinosaurs with long neck, small head and long tail

scavenger animal that feeds on (dead) meat which it finds, rather than hunts

scutes bony protective plates offering defence against attack

semi-bipedal sometimes walks on hind legs, at other times walks on all fours

species a category of living things, plants or animals, refers to related living things capable of breeding with one another to produce young

stegosaurs a group of herbivorous dinosaurs of the Jurassic and early Cretaceous periods, predominantly living in North America and China.

tendons connect muscle to bone

territory the land or area where an animal lives

thecodonts ancestors of the dinosaurs

theropods fast moving, bipedal carnivores with grasping hands and claws

tibia shin-bone

tree fern fern with a central trunk

trackways footprints preserved in rock as fossils

triassic first period of the Mesozoic era, 248–203 million years ago

vertebrae the bones which are linked together to make the spine of an animal

vertebrate animal with a backbone

warm-blooded able to keep the body at constant temperature, regardless of the environment

INDEX

INDEX

INDEX

ACKNOWLEDGEMENTS

The authors and publishers would like to thank the following people who played such a significant role in creating this Dinosaur Encyclopedia:

Illustration
HL Studios

Page Design
HL Studios

Editorial
Jennifer Clark, Lucie Williams

Photo Research
Sam Morley

Project Management
HL Studios

Jacket Design
JPX

Production
Elaine Ward

All photographs and other illustrations are copyright of USGS, istockphoto, stockxpert, stockxchnge, Flickr.com, except where stated below:

THE NATURAL HISTORY MUSEUM, LONDON

FOSSILISED DINOSAUR HEART © JIM PAGE / NORTH CAROLINA MUSEUM OF NATURAL SCIENCES / SCIENCE PHOTO LIBRARY

DINOSAUR EXTINCTION © VICTOR HABBICK VISIONS / SCIENCE PHOTO LIBRARY

CONSTRUCTION OF A REPLICA SKELETON OF TITANOSAURUS © PHILIPPE PLAILLY / SCIENCE PHOTO LIBRARY

FOSSILISED HEAD OF CYNOGNATHUS CRATERNOTUS © SINCLAIR STAMMERS / SCIENCE PHOTO LIBRARY

DINOSAUR TRACKS © OMIKRON / SCIENCE PHOTO LIBRARY

SONAR IMAGE OF LOCH NESS MONSTER © MIRRORPIX

BARNEY THE PURPLE DINOSAUR © REUTERS/CORBIS

FLINTSTONES © CAPITAL PICTURES

"HADROSAURUS" BRONZE SCULPTURE BY JOHN GIANNOTTI 2003

A Belani, Belgianchocolate, Bernard Price Institute for Palaeontological Research Adam Morrel, Kaptain Kobold, Kevinzim, Sarah Montani, Lawrence M. Witmer, PhD, Natuurhistorisch Museum Rotterdam (http://www.nmr.nl/), Striatic, Mark Klingler/Carnegie Museum of Natural History, John Sibbick Illustration, Musée d'histoire naturelle de Fribourg, Suisse, Jarbewowski, Maidstone Borough Council, The Academy of Natural Sciences Philadelphia.